KEITH CHEETHAM's interest in the Pilgrim Fathers began over twenty years ago when, as Sheffield's first Conference and Tourist Officer, he devised a national Mayflower Trail for the tourist industry. This was a detailed broadsheet designed for North American visitors giving information about the Pilgrim Fathers in England. It was a guide to many of the important sites where the Pilgrims originated and explaining how the Separatist movement started. It also specified some of the many places connected with the Pilgrims and their courageous efforts to find religious freedom outwith their native land, first in Holland, then the New World. Thousands of copies of the broadsheet were distributed to visitors by the American Embassy in London.

In 1988 Keith was invited to set up a unit to market and develop England's Black Country as a tourist destination, a post he held until 1997 when he formed his own tourism consultancy, based in Wolverhampton. Having travelled extensively in Europe and North America, some of his creative initiatives in the tourism field have gained international recognition.

A playwright and regular broadcaster on BBC Radio, he is the author of two books on Mary Queen of Scots – *Mary Queen of Scots – The Captive Years* and *On the Trail of Mary Queen of Scots* – the latter first published by Luath Press Limited in June 1999. Using his wide knowledge of the Tudor, Elizabethan and Jacobean periods and the Pilgrim Fathers, this book is written in an uncomplicated style. The publication should prove an invaluable guide and asset to any visitor who wishes to follow the trail of America's founding fathers.

Now available in Luath's *On the Trail of* series

To Lilian,

On the Trail of
The Pilgrim Fathers

With my very best wishes

Keith

J. KEITH CHEETHAM

(J. Keith Cheetham)

Luath Press Limited

EDINBURGH

www.luath.co.uk

april 2001

First Published 2001

The paper used in this book is neutral-sized and recyclable. It is made from elemental chlorine-free pulps sourced from renewable forests.

Printed and bound by IBT Global, London and New York

Typeset in 10.5 point Sabon by
Senga Fairgrieve, Edinburgh, 0131 658 1763

He who would valiant be
'Gainst all disaster,
Let him in constancy
    Follow the Master.
There's no discouragement
Shall make him once relent
His first avowed intent
    To be a pilgrim.

Since, Lord, thou dost defend
Us with thy Spirit,
We know we at the end
    Shall life inherit.
Then fancies flee away!
I'll fear not what men say,
I'll labour night and day
    To be a pilgrim.

John Bunyan, 1628-88

*This book is dedicated to my grandson,
Oliver J. Dene, in the hope that he also will be given courage,
faith, strength and vision on his own pilgrimage through life.*

Acknowledgements

I have received an enormous amount of help, guidance and assistance from many people and organisations during my researches and compilation of this book. In particular, I would like to single out just a few who have given of their time to help, without whose wise counselling, factual information or checking of the manuscript, I could not have completed the job.

I owe a special debt of appreciation to the following friends – Lilian Cameron, Roger Gilbride; Margaret & Michael Hides, Patricia Key and Anne I. Taylor; to my colleagues in the tourism industry – Patrick C. Apel (Plymouth County Convention & Visitors Bureau, USA), Andrew Crabtree (Boston Guildhall Museum), Malcolm J Dolby MA, (Bassetlaw Museums), Edward Gregory (Essex County Council – Enterprise), Barry Higham (Boston Borough Council), Linda Maiden (New Jersey Office of Travel & Tourism, USA) and Dr. Peter Roberts (Plymouth Marketing Bureau). In the same context, I should also mention the kind assistance I have received from Tourist Information Centres in the following places – Atherstone, Boston, Dartmouth, Droitwich, Harwich, Plymouth, Retford, Tamworth, Totnes, Southwark, Wigan, Worksop and Wrexham. The VVV Tourist Office in Leiden, Netherlands have also been extremely helpful. An especial word of thanks is due to Dr. Jeremy Bangs for checking my manuscript. Jeremy is not only the Director of the Leiden American Pilgrim Museum in the Netherlands but also former Chief Curator of Plimoth Plantation and visiting Curator of Manuscripts at the Pilgrim Hall Museum of the Pilgrim Society, both in Plymouth, Massachusetts.

Other bodies or individuals have included – Amsterdam Historic Museum; Audrey Bateman, Canterbury; Mrs. D.A. Davies, All Saints Church, Babworth; staff at Gainsborough Old Hall; Philip Glover, Mayflower Inn, Rotherhithe; Essex Record Office; clergy and staff of Lincoln Cathedral; New Jersey Commerce & Economic Growth Commission, USA; Netherlands Maritime Museum, Amsterdam; Reverend Nicholas Richards, rector, St. Mary's Church, Rotherhithe; Andy Rutter, Harwich Society, clergy and staff of Southwark Cathedral; Southwark Local Studies Library; Rosemary Switzer, Princeton University, New Jersey, USA; Wigan History Shop and Wolverhampton Local History and Archives Department.

Finally, I should like to single out my colleague, David Middleton, for his line drawings; Jim Lewis, cartographer; Catriona Scott, editor; Tom Bee; and my publishers at Luath Press Limited, Audrey and Gavin MacDougall, who again have given me unstinting support and encouragement in this my second publication for their organisation.

Contents

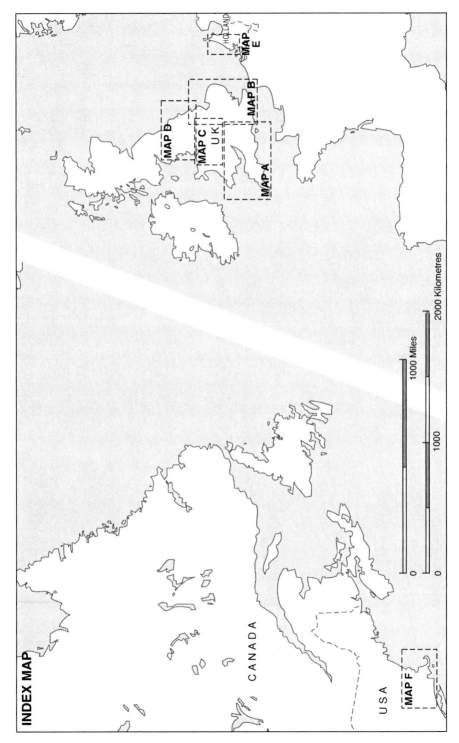

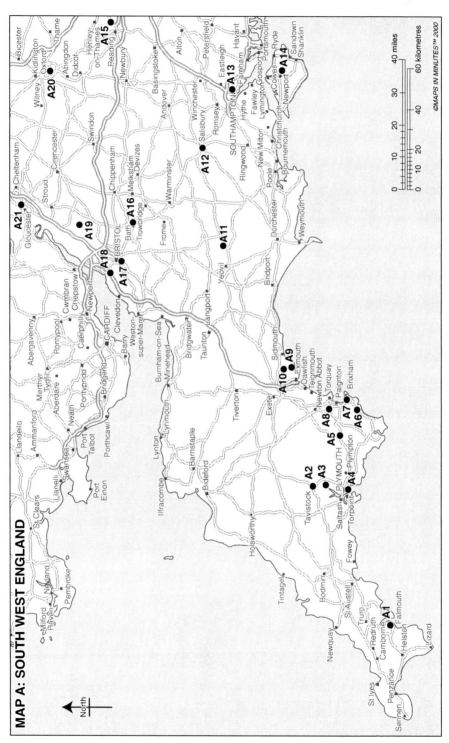

MAP A: SOUTH WEST ENGLAND

x

Key to Map A: South West England

Ref	Page(s)

A1 – Falmouth 46
Captain Bartholomew Gosnold sailed from Falmouth harbour on an expedition to the New World in 1602.

A2 – Tavistock 15
Sir Francis Drake was born in 1540 at a farmstead near the Devonshire town of Tavistock.

A3 – Buckland Abbey NT 18
A later home of Sir Francis Drake, situated in a secluded valley above the River Tavy in Devon. *Drake's Drum* is one of the artefacts on display.

A4 – Plymouth 15
Final departure point of the Pilgrim Fathers on the *Mayflower* on 6 September 1620.

A5 - Totnes 68
Small town on River Dart. An Elizabethan market is held every Tuesday during the summer.

A6 – Dartmouth and Kingswear 67,68
The *Mayflower* and *Speedwell* put into Dartmouth harbour when the latter sprang a leak. It had to be repaired and caused further delay before the Pilgrim Fathers could leave England for the New World. Kingswear Castle can be seen on the opposite side of the river.

A7 – Brixham 55,98
A replica of the *Mayflower* was built in Upland's Yard in 1955 and, two years later, followed the same journey across the Atlantic as the original ship. The prototype was named *Mayflower II* and is permanently moored in the harbour at Plymouth, Massachusetts.

A8 – Compton Castle NT 19,20
Ancestral home of explorer, Sir Humphrey Gilbert, situated near Paignton.

A9 – Budleigh Salterton 20
The Octagon was the home of British artist, Sir John Millais who painted *The Boyhood of Raleigh*.

A10 – Hayes Barton and East Budleigh 10,20
Sir Walter Raleigh was born in a substantial house at Hayes Barton in 1552. The Raleigh family pew can be seen at nearby All Saints Parish Church in East Budleigh.

A11 – Sherborne Castle EH **and Abbey** 22
A new Sherborne Castle was built by Sir Walter Raleigh in the 1590s. The old castle was destroyed by Cromwell during the Civil War (now an English Heritage site). The nearby Sherborne Abbey dates back to Saxon times.

A12 – Salisbury and Cathedral 21
Sir Walter Raleigh stayed at the White Hart Inn after his failed venture at the Orinoco river. Salisbury Cathedral has a number of American connections.

A13 – Southampton 58,63
Original rendez-vous point of *Mayflower* with *Speedwell*..

A14 – Carisbrooke Castle, Isle of Wight EH 63,126
Charles I was imprisoned at the castle prior to his trial and execution in London in 1649.

A15 – Twyford 137
William Penn died in 1718 at his home in nearby Field Ruscombe (now demolished).

A16 – Claverton Manor near Bath 151
Home of Britain's first American Museum, opened in 1961.

A17 – Bristol 11
Port from where early explorers left for the New World. John Wesley built his first Methodist place of worship, the 'New Room', in the Broadmead in 1739.

A18 – Pill 148
Small port near mouth of River Avon near Bristol. Departure point to New World of Methodist preacher, Francis Asbury, in 1771.

A19 – Wotton-under-Edge 79
Home of *Mayflower* passenger, Stephen Hopkins.

A20 – Oxford 32
Oxford colleges were 'hotbeds' of Nonconformism. John and Charles Wesley, George Whitefield and others formed the 'Holy Club', the forerunner of the Methodist movement.

A21 – Gloucester 144
George Whitefield, Methodist preacher, was born at the Old Bell Inn in 1714. His family worshipped at St. Mary de Crypt church where he was baptised.

Abbreviations

EH   English Heritage
NT   National Trust (England)

Addresses for the above organisations can be found on pages 153 and 154.

The page number given for each location on this map and the maps which follow is the first page on which reference is made to that location.

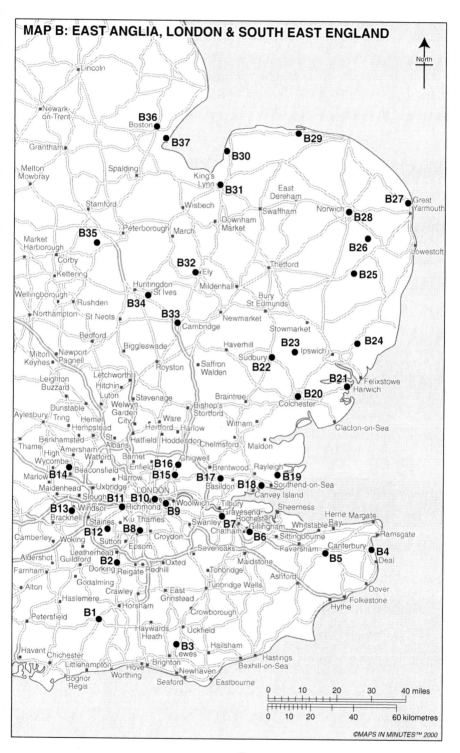

MAP B: EAST ANGLIA, LONDON & SOUTH EAST ENGLAND

Key to Map B: East Anglia, London & South East England

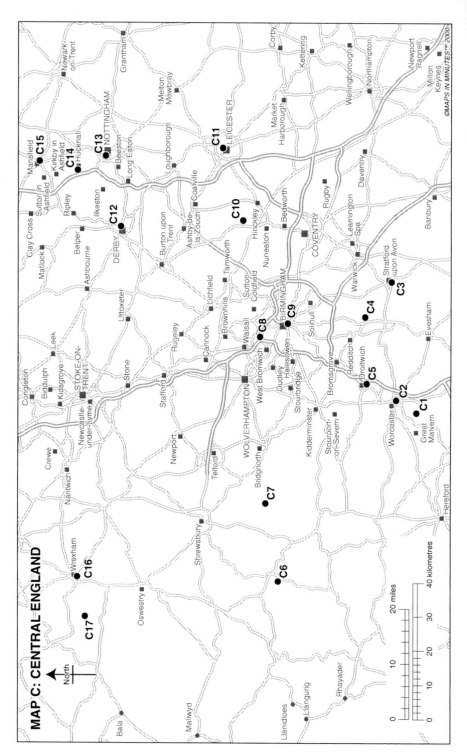

MAP C: CENTRAL ENGLAND

©MAPS IN MINUTES™ 2000

Key to Map C: Central England

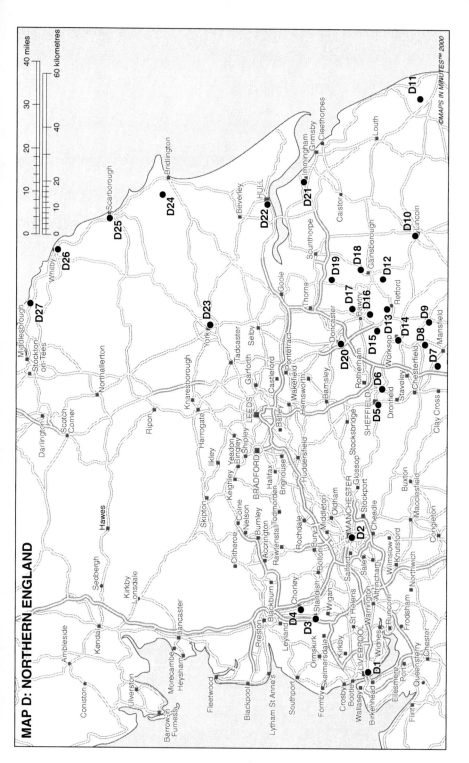

MAP D: NORTHERN ENGLAND

©MAPS IN MINUTES™ 2000

Key to Map D: Northern England

Ref   Page(s)   Ref   Page(s)

D1 – Liverpool   11
Port from where thousands of British emigrants departed for the New World.

D2 – Manchester   138
The sect known as 'Shaking' Quakers originated in the city.

D3 – Standish – St. Wilfrid's Church   45
The church has a Standish chapel.

D4 – Chorley – St. Lawrence`s Church and Duxbury Hall   45
Traditionally church where Miles Standish was baptised but not proven. The hall was once owned by the Standish family.

D5 – Sheffield Manor and Paradise Square   28
Cardinal Wolsey was taken ill at the Manor. John Wesley preached in the square to his largest weekday congregation in July 1779.

D6 – Handsworth – St. Mary's Church, and Ballifield Hall, Sheffield   133
Mahlon Stacye was baptised in the church in 1638. His home was at Ballifield until leaving for the New World in 1678.

D7 – Hardwick Hall *NT* **and Old Hardwick Hall** *EH*   22
Birthplace and home of Bess of Hardwick, Countess of Shrewsbury.

D8 – Warsop   26
Former home of Anne Stuffen, wife of Reverend Richard Clyfton.

D9 – Edwinstowe and Major Oak   31
Robin Hood links.

D10 – Lincoln Cathedral and Castle   25,36,48
Cathedral has links with Captain John Smith, explorer. The Pilgrims stood trial at the castle after their first abortive attempt to escape to Holland.

D11 – Willoughby – St. Helene's Church   46
Captain John Smith was born in the village and baptised in the church.

D12 – Sturton-le-Steeple – Church of St. Peter & St. Paul   31
Early Separatists John Smyth and John Robinson were both born in the village.

D13 – Babworth – All Saints Church and Retford   25,26
Church is considered to have been the birthplace of the Pilgrim movement when Reverend Richard Clyfton was rector.

D14 – Worksop Museum   31
The museum houses a comprehensive display about the Pilgrim Fathers.

D15 – Blyth   30
The Church of St. Helena at Austerfield was annexed to the Priory at Blyth.

D16 – Scrooby – St. Wilfrid's Church and Scrooby Manor   26,28
The Manor was home to William Brewster and an early meeting place for Separatists.

D17 – Bawtry and Austerfield – Church of St. Helena   27,29,38
Birthplace of William Bradford who was baptised in the church in 1589.

D18 – Gainsborough – Old Hall   25
Early meeting place of Separatists under John Smyth.

D19 – Epworth – Old Rectory   144
Birthplace of John and Charles Wesley.

D20 – Doncaster   49
Birthplace of John Carver, Pilgrim leader, circa 1575.

D21 – Killingholme Creek   38
Departure point of Pilgrim men on south bank of River Humber in their second attempt to reach Holland.

D22 – Hull   38
William Brewster made arrangements in Hull for a ship to take the Pilgrims on their second attempt to reach Holland.

D23 – York   34
William Brewster appeared before magistrates and fined £20 for disobeying Church authorities.

D24 – Boynton Hall and Church of St. Andrew   12
Home of William Strickland, first Englishman to set foot on American soil.

D25 – Scarborough Castle *EH*   12,132
William Strickland was the town's MP. George Fox was imprisoned in the castle for his Nonconformist preaching.

D26 – Whitby – St. Hilda's Abbey   29
Conference held in 664 AD to Romanise the Church's calendar.

D27 — Marske-by-the-Sea   11
Boyhood home of William Strickland.

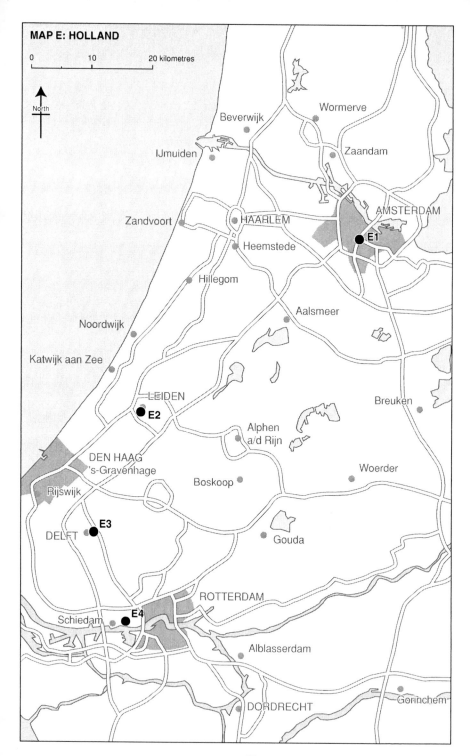

Key to Map E: Holland

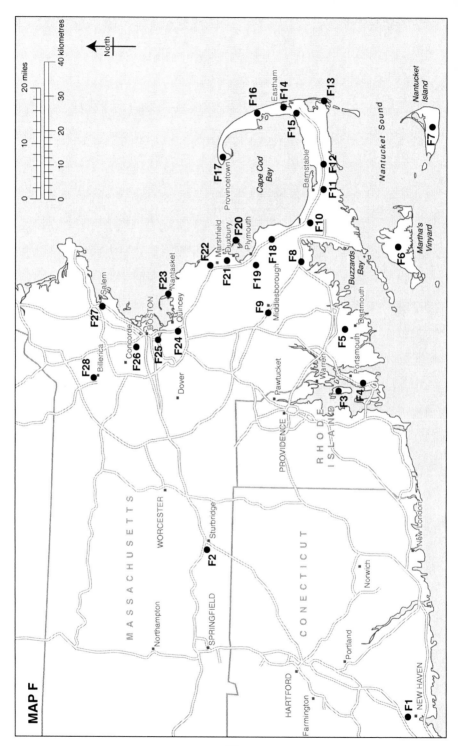

MAP F

North

20 miles
40 kilometres

MASSACHUSETTS

Northampton
SPRINGFIELD
WORCESTER
Sturbridge
F2

Billerica
F28
Concorde
F26
F25
Dover
BOSTON
Salem
F27
Quincey
F24
Nantasket
F23
F22
Marshfield
Duxbury
F21 F20
Plymouth
Middlesborough
F19
F9
F8
F18
F17
Provincetown
Cape Cod Bay
F16
Eastham
F14
F15
Barnstable
F13
F11 F12
F10
Buzzards Bay
F5
Portsmouth
Dartmouth
F4
F3
Warren
Pawtucket
PROVIDENCE
R H O D E   I S L A N D

Nantucket Sound
Martha's Vinyard
F6
Nantucket Island
F7

C O N E C T I C U T
Portland
Norwich
New London
Farmington
HARTFORD
NEW HAVEN
F1

xx

Key to Map F: New England

Locations situated in Massachusetts unless otherwise stated.

Foreword

MY INTEREST IN THE Pilgrim Fathers was first aroused when I was a boy after an outing from Sheffield to the small town of Bawtry in South Yorkshire, close to its border with Nottinghamshire. It is a lovely old place with a number of Georgian buildings straggling along what was once the Great North Road between London and Scotland before a modern by-pass was built. South of the town is an inn called *The Pilgrim Fathers* and I was curious to know what those most revered gentlemen had to do with that area. 'Surely they came from Plymouth?' I thought to myself. I soon discovered that a number of the Pilgrims had not only been born and bred in the region but also an important branch of the Separatist movement had started there.

Years later, as Conference and Tourist Officer for the City of Sheffield, I was seeking a suitable subject to attract North American visitors. Knowing of the nearby 'Pilgrim' links, I started to research the subject and, with encouragement from the British Tourist Authority, set about compiling a national *Mayflower Trail*. The idea was to both describe and link up many of the important centres connected with the Pilgrims' story in England. I also contacted the Mayflower Descendants Society in Massachusetts who proved extremely helpful. Yet, I soon found that my research took me beyond the era of the original Pilgrim Fathers to the time of earlier explorers and also some of the settlers who followed the Pilgrims across the Atlantic ocean.

During my travels in North America, I discovered more about what happened to these people once they left British shores. In many cases, they left a legacy to the American nation upon which part of its national identity has been founded.

The story of the Pilgrim Fathers and those who came after is exciting. Though they are generally described as 'Pilgrim Fathers', let us not forget that they also included wives and children who had to shoulder the same perils, trials and hardships. It is a tale of brave folk who, with sheer determination and trust in God, managed to overcome difficulties, storms and tragedies to become the founders of a mighty nation.

J. Keith Cheetham
March 2001

Introduction

THE PILGRIM FATHERS STAND out in history as the best remembered of all American colonists and over one million North Americans count them as their ancestors. The Pilgrims were the first group to found their own colony and run it on a system of administration and obedience which was to be the forerunner of the established American tradition of government. Yet who were these men and women and where did the name 'Pilgrim Fathers' originate?

Emigration to North America started in the early 16th century with explorers such as Christopher Columbus. Britain was a land in religious turmoil as successive monarchs alternated between the Roman Catholic and Protestant faiths. Under Queen Elizabeth I the country was Protestant and the Church of England was the Established Church. By and large, the population were forced to accept the Church of England's authority. Those who refused suffered persecution. Some simply wanted to 'purify' the Church by scrapping the prayer book in favour of the Bible and also discard the ceremonial aspects of worship. These people were called 'Puritans'. They also wanted to do away with the government of the Church of England by the bishops and clergy and replace them with ministers and elders.

There were several types of 'Puritans' and, in general, we follow one specific group called 'Separatists' who mainly originated from areas in the English counties of Nottinghamshire, Lincolnshire and Yorkshire. Once having decided to 'separate' from the practices of the Church of England, they soon became a target for suppression and ridicule. Seeking freedom to live and worship according to their own faith, the Separatists fled to Holland. They spent a year in Amsterdam before they moved to Leiden where they stayed for nearly twelve years. They became restless and finally decided upon a course which would lead them across the Atlantic on the ship called the *Mayflower* leaving Plymouth on 6 September 1620 bound for a new life in the New World.

Although the name 'Pilgrimes' appears in William Bradford's history, *Of Plymouth Plantation*, it was not used by the Separatists themselves. It was given to the 'forefathers of New England' during the 1840s when there was much enthusiasm for these early colonists. Even so, they were 'Pilgrims' to a new land and their story is one of great danger, tragedy, determination, bravery and a strong faith in God to see them to their destiny. When the *Mayflower* first arrived at Cape Cod on 11 November 1620 after a hazardous voyage across an angry ocean, their troubles were far from over. Yet the Pilgrims persevered, despite losing nearly half of their original group of 102 within the first year due to illness and extreme weather conditions. They had many adventures and suffered great hardships before their settlement was finally established at Plimoth Plantation. The Pilgrim Fathers were a role model for thousands of settlers who arrived in America over the next few years.

Many who followed in the footsteps of the Pilgrim Fathers also went to escape religious bigotry, to further their ambitions, or for family reasons. Some went to help with the colonisation of the New World whilst others simply crossed the Atlantic to spread the Gospel of Jesus Christ. These settlers became part of what is known as the 'second wave of Pilgrims' who made an important contribution in both creating and building the American way of life. The stories of some of these other pioneers and benefactors are included in the book. Collectively, each helped fulfil the idealistic ambitions of the early Pilgrims. They were not only to create a new country but also to lead and govern it.

Principal Personae

EARLY EXPLORERS

Henry the Navigator, Christopher Columbus, Vasco da Gama, John & Sebastian Cabot, William Strickland, Ferdinand Magellan, Sir John Hawkins, Sir Francis Drake, Martin Frobisher, Sir Humphrey Gilbert, Sir Walter Raleigh, Sir Richard Grenville, Captain John Smith and Captain Bartholomew Gosnold.

MERCHANT ADVENTURERS

Thomas Weston, Christopher Martin and Thomas Goff.

SHIPS' CAPTAINS AND CREW

Mayflower – Captain Christopher Jones, John Clarke, Richard Clarke and Robert Coppin.
Speedwell – Captain Reynolds

PILGRIM FATHERS

John Alden, Isaac Allerton, John Billington, William & Mary Bradford, William & Mary Brewster, John & Catherine Carver, James & Mary Chilton, Francis Cooke, Edward Fuller, Dr. Samuel Fuller, Stephen Hopkins, John Howland, Captain Miles and Rose Standish, Edward Tilley and Edward Winslow.

OTHER SEPARATISTS

Thomas Brewer, Robert Browne, Reverend Richard Clyfton, Francis Johnson, Pastor John Robinson, John Smyth and John Winthrop.

NATIVE AMERICAN INDIANS

Samoset, Squanto, Massasoit and Hobomok.

LATER PIONEERS AND BENEFACTORS

George Fox, Mahlon Stacye, William Penn, Elihu Yale, John Harvard, John & Charles Wesley, George Whitefield, Bishop Francis Asbury and Roger Williams.

(The above lists are by no means comprehensive but refer to those mentioned principally within the text of the book. See Chapter 8 for a detailed summary of the *Mayflower* passengers.)

CHAPTER I

Columbus and the Early Explorers

NORTH AND SOUTH AMERICA are old in time and, as far as can be ascertained, settlers first reached the New World 30,000 to 40,000 years ago, perhaps even earlier. It is generally thought that people from Asia first populated North America during an ice age which caused a natural bridge to form between Alaska and Siberia. In particular, the Incas, aboriginal Peruvian Indians, the Aztec who founded the Mexican Empire centuries before their conquest by the Spaniards under Hernan Cortes in 1519, and the Maya in Central America, built their own rich cultures which laid an early foundation for the New World.

By the 15th century there were around 500 tribes of North American Indians. Some of their names live on in the various states – Illinois, Alabama and Iowa. However, there were probably no more than a million of these people whereas it is thought that there were at least fifteen million living in Central and South America. With the coming of settlers from Western Europe, their world was gradually eroded as they were driven westwards and their lands taken over by explorers, exploiters and colonists.

One of the earliest explorers who ventured into the Atlantic was Henry the Navigator (1394-1460), a prince of Portugal, who had seen cargoes arriving from Asia. He sailed down the West African coast in 1420 but, due to violent Atlantic storms and sea currents, was driven to the Madeira islands. In 1431 he reached the Azores and established a base for further expeditions and by 1460 his ships had sailed down the African coast as far as Sierra Leone.

Perhaps the most famous explorer to head westwards was Christopher Columbus (1451-1506). His birthplace was probably Genoa, Italy, about 1451. In 1476 he sailed on a convoy to France and the Baltic. The convoy was attacked by French ships off the

Straits of Gibraltar and Columbus had to swim to safety as his boat sank. He eventually reached Lisbon where he stayed with his brother, Bartolomé, who was working there. He settled in Lisbon and married well into one of Portugal's first families. He later lived in Porto Santo in the Madeira islands and had a son, Diego. Columbus's work as a sea captain took him on a number of voyages to the African coast in search of gold.

Columbus approached King John of Portugal for financial backing and assistance to head westwards across the Atlantic believing that he would discover the Far East when he reached the other side of the ocean. The King refused and Columbus was referred to the Council for Geographical Affairs who also turned down the application. Frustrated, he turned to the Spanish monarchs, Ferdinand and Isabella who, though doubtful about the proposal, were finally persuaded to sponsor Columbus in 1492. Ferdinand II (1452-1516), King of Aragon from 1479, had married his cousin Isabella I (1451-1504) who had succeeded to the throne of Castile in 1474 thus uniting these two important kingdoms. Their youngest daughter was Catherine of Aragon, the first wife of Henry VIII of England.

Columbus set out with three galleons, the *Santa Maria*, the *Niña* and the *Pinta*, sailing slowly in a south-westerly direction from Spain, carried by the winds and currents. Despite a sometimes mutinous crew, Columbus persevered. Had they thought that a supposed voyage of 2,500 miles (4,000 kilometres) would extend to over 12,000 miles (19,000 kilometres), many of the crew would never have undertaken it. As an inducement, Columbus offered a reward of 10,000 Spanish maravedis (a

The *Santa Maria*

Spanish copper coin worth less than a farthing in English currency prior to decimalisation) to the man who first sighted land. (He later claimed the 10,000 maravedis for himself saying that he was the first person to have sighted land.) According to his reckoning, they were about 2,100 miles (3,360 kilometres) west of the Canary Islands when a pelican was spotted, followed, a few days later, by flocks of other birds. One of the crew found a branch of a tree floating on the water. Next day, a sailor in the 'crow's nest' of the *Pinta* sighted land and the three Spanish ships set a course which was to take them not only to dry land but also into the history books of maritime culture. A few hours later, they anchored off a small island which was named by Columbus 'San Salvador' (in English 'Holy or Blessed Saviour') in thankfulness of their deliverance. San Salvador is in the Bahamas. The date was 12 October 1492 and Columbus claimed the island for the Spanish monarchs and reported that the natives bowed in allegiance.

The ships sailed on and discovered the island of Cuba which they were delighted to learn was rich in gold and, again, the natives appeared friendly. However, on reaching the island which Columbus named 'Hispaniola', they found the locals were far more aggressive. Columbus ordered the construction of a fort which he named as 'Puerto de Navidad' (Port of the Nativity). Forty crew members volunteered to stay and man it, and to hunt for gold.

The *Niña* and the *Pinta* headed back across the Atlantic to report their findings to the Spanish king and queen. They met with violent storms and were badly blown off course and separated. The *Niña* finally arrived in Portugal on 18 February 1493 and Columbus and his crew were received by King John. Columbus in triumph proceeded to the Spanish court where there were great celebrations.

Though it is said that Columbus discovered America, this is not true. The two continents and their associated islands had been occupied for thousands of years by Indians. Norsemen had made a landfall on Nova Scotia around 1000 AD.

Columbus's final journey was to San Domingo in 1504 and he died two years later, according to popular theory at Valladolid in

Spain. His actual place of burial is still open to conjecture. The cathedrals at Seville in Spain and at Santo Domingo in the West Indies both lay claim to his relics.

Vasco da Gama (1460-1521) was a Portuguese explorer, born in the small seaport of Sines. In July 1497 he set off on a voyage southwards along the coast of Africa. In order to avoid the doldrums and the Guinea current, he navigated his ships to the south and west, returning to the coast close to the Cape of Good Hope. By April 1498, they had reached the coast of Kenya where they were given a friendly reception by the king. They then headed east across the Indian Ocean and reached Calicut in southern India. In September 1499 Vasco da Gama returned to Portugal where he was much feted for having established a new trading route to the Indies, bringing back precious goods and treasures. Da Gama was granted the title 'Admiral of the Seas of the Indies'. He is generally acknowledged as the first explorer to have rounded the treacherous Cape of Good Hope.

By the end of the 15th century other nations were greedily eyeing the newly-discovered lands which Spain and Portugal had opened up. England's King Henry VII sponsored two expeditions to the North Atlantic coast by the explorer, John Cabot (1450-1499) and his son, Sebastian (1476-1557). Cabot was an Italian from Venice (his name is the anglicised version of Giovanni Caboto). The Cabots and their crew sailed westwards from Bristol (A17) in the *Matthew* on 2 May 1497 and within four weeks had discovered land, which they thought at the time was part of Asia, and named it Newfoundland, claiming it for the English sovereign.

In 1498 John Cabot set off from Bristol on another journey and reached the island mass of Greenland and sailed southwards by Labrador and on to Nova Scotia. Then he travelled down the coast of North America and headed back across the Atlantic to report his findings to King Henry VII. In 1509 his son, Sebastian Cabot, set out across the Atlantic in search of a north-west Passage to Asia and sailed into Hudson Bay through the Hudson Strait, hitherto undiscovered territory.

Whereas Columbus had opened up the riches of Central and

South America for the Spaniards, John Cabot discovered for England the rich fishing grounds off Newfoundland. He was honoured by King Henry and became a national hero, especially in Bristol. In 1897, the Cabot Tower was erected in Bristol (A17) to commemorate the 400th anniversary of John Cabot's discovery of Newfoundland. It stands high above the city in a prominent position in parkland which looks down towards the harbour from which the explorers set sail on their historic journeys to the New World.

Bristol's growth as a port was not only due to a good defensive position but also its safe harbour and it was the starting point for a number of exploratory ventures to North America and the West Indies. Its trade in the Middle Ages was mainly with Ireland and importing wine from France, which has continued to the present. The 15th century brought about an expansion in trade with Spain and Portugal. Bristol became notorious when it became involved in the slave trade. After the American War of Independence, Bristol went into decline and business was transferred to other west coast ports such as Liverpool (D1) and Glasgow. In recent years the harbour has been re-vitalised and it continues to service smaller vessels. In 1970 the *Great Britain* was returned from the Falkland Islands and is being fully restored to its former glory.

The diocese of Bristol was inaugurated in 1542 by Henry VIII with the abbey church of St. Augustine as the cathedral. Many churches were built including the magnificent St. Mary Redcliffe, described by Queen Elizabeth 1 on her visit to the church in 1574 as 'the fairest, goodliest and most famous parisch church in England'. It is one of the largest and finest Gothic churches in the country mainly due to the generosity of local merchants whose fortunes were made through trading fleets based in the nearby harbour.

One of Sebastian Cabot's crew was William Strickland, a navigator, who came from Marske (D27) in the North Riding of Yorkshire and is generally considered to have been the first Englishman to set foot on American soil. The ship returned with the first turkeys ever seen in Europe. By tradition, young

Strickland looked after the turkeys on the voyage home and, years later, when he was granted a coat of arms in 1550, he chose as his crest 'a turkey-cock in its pride proper'. The original drawing for the crest, still held at the College of Arms, is the oldest picture of a turkey known to exist. By 1549 Strickland had done well enough to purchase the manor of Boynton (D24) near Bridlington in East Yorkshire, together with other nearby estates. In Boynton, he dismantled the Norman manor house and replaced it with Boynton Hall, which although altered and added to since, is still substantially the house he built. He later became the Member of Parliament for Scarborough (D25) and died in 1598. Boynton Hall is still occupied by one of his descendants.

Around the same time as the Cabot voyages, another Italian, Amerigo Vespucci, led naval expeditions to the eastern coast of South America. His claim that he had arrived at a new continent prompted the geographer, Martin Waldseemüller, in 1507 to suggest that this new country should be named as the 'land of Americus', after its discoverer. This is disputed by some, as the Sheriff of Bristol at the time of Cabot's expedition was a man named Richard Amerycke and it has been said that the new continent was named after him and not Amerigo Vespucci. The matter is still open to debate.

One of the most important journeys of exploration was made between 1519 and 1521 when the Portuguese navigator, Ferdinand Magellan (1480-1521), under the auspices of the Spanish monarch, Charles 1, proved that there was a western sea route to the Indies. Magellan was known as a hard taskmaster and ruthless in his punishment of mutineers. One was even skinned alive.

Magellan set off from Cadiz in September 1519 in a southerly direction, passing the west coast of Africa, and headed for the tip of South America. His fleet of five ships sailed through the treacherous channel which was later named the Magellan Straits and crossed the Pacific reaching the Philippines in April 1521. In a skirmish with hostile natives Magellan was killed. In 1522 one of his protégés, Juan Sebastián del Cano, headed across the Indian

Ocean to the Cape of Good Hope and back to Spain, thus completing the circumnavigation of the globe begun by Magellan and proving that the world was round.

Spain continued with its conquests of Central and South America and seized Mexico and its treasures from the Aztec. The Inca empire was also defeated and the gold and other treasures were sent back to Spain, increasing the national wealth, and, in turn, providing finance for new seafaring schemes. The Spanish stopped at nothing in their bid for New World supremacy. It was a struggle that would eventually lead to war between England and Spain.

CHAPTER 2

In Good Queen Bess's Glorious Days!

WHEN HENRY VIII BROKE with the Church of Rome and established himself as head of the Church of England, he angered countries such as France, Portugal and Spain, and caused religious and civil unrest in England. Unrest continued as England's monarchs changed the country's religion according to their own faith and people were increasingly persecuted for their beliefs. Religious dissension spread.

Until the Elizabethan period, seafaring expeditions by England were not much encouraged. It was in the reign of 'Good Queen Bess', as Elizabeth I was affectionately known, that England's seafaring prowess came into its own. It was an age of discovery and is often referred to as the 'Golden Years' of England's supremacy on the high seas. There was keen competition between European countries in search of new lands and wealth. The Spanish and Portuguese had established colonies, especially in the West Indies and Central and South America. Countries such as England, France and the Low Countries were clamouring to take their share of the new wealth and economic expansion provided through the setting up of new trade routes. It was a time of high drama around the Atlantic and Pacific shores as one country vied with another to gain control. This was the era of heroic admirals, bold buccaneers, pirates, castaways, shipwrecks, gold doubloons and hidden treasure.

The great seafarers combined their role of statesmen with that of profes-

Queen Elizabeth I

sional adventurers, renowned for their leadership in battle. A steady stream of brave entrepreneurs helped Britain become one of the greatest and most powerful countries.

With the discovery of the African continent came the degrading traffic in slaves. One of the earliest slave traders was Sir John Hawkins (1532-1595) from Plymouth (A4) who took 400 West African slaves across the Atlantic in 1564 to sell to sugar planters. They were bartered for and sold like any other commercial commodity, herded like cattle into uncomfortable and insanitary accommodation on board ship, often being shackled in irons, starved and ill-treated to ensure they caused the minimum of trouble on the long journey.

Hawkins sailed westwards again in 1567 in the ship *Judith*. On this voyage he took with him his young cousin, Francis Drake (1540-1596), who was fast making a name for himself as a daring seafarer and adventurer.

There was little love lost between England and Spain on the high seas, though diplomatic relationships on land were not under the same strain. Queen Elizabeth preferred to avoid open conflict and thus turned a blind eye to the activities of her sea captains, prefering them to become privateers on more or less an independent basis. This was really a crafty way of encouraging, but not being seen to be supporting, piracy. The English were envious of the rewards the Spaniards were reaping in the Caribbean islands and Central and South America. They therefore lost no opportunity to plunder and capture any Spanish ship. Through this type of action, Drake got a taste for the life which was to bring him fame and fortune as a national hero.

Francis Drake was born into a Protestant family at a farmstead in Crowndale near the Devonshire town of Tavistock (A2). During a period of religious persecutions, his father, Edmund Drake, was hounded out of Devon and the family fled to Gillingham (B6) in Kent. They set up home in the hull of an old ship and Edmund became a preacher to workers in the local shipbuilding yards, the forerunner of Chatham Naval Dockyard (B6), now an excellent maritime tourist attraction on the North Kent coast. Edmund later became vicar of the nearby village of Upchurch (B6). These boyhood experiences of Francis Drake and the talk he would have heard from seafaring folk about the Spanish threat to England made a marked impression upon him.

Drake became a pirate, working for his country and attacking Spanish ships as they sailed to and from the West Indies and the Spanish Main. In 1577 he was given a golden opportunity when he was commissioned by Queen Elizabeth to lead an expedition to the South Seas to attack Spanish territories. He set out from Plymouth with a fleet of five ships, headed by the *Pelican*. It was to be a four-year voyage which would bring him great wealth and ensure his place in English history books. It was also a great boost for the English Queen.

By the time Drake sailed through the Straits of Magellan and into the Pacific the only ship left of the original five was the *Pelican* which Drake renamed the *Golden Hind*. Drake charted a course northwards and headed along the Chilean coast. En route, they lost no opportunity to plunder any Spanish ship or town they chanced upon. The *Golden Hind* continued up the west coast of North America until it reached what is today known as San Francisco Bay. Drake claimed the land for Queen Elizabeth, founded a colony and named it New Albion.

Drake set off across the Pacific. By October 1579, he had arrived in the Philippines and from there travelled to Ternate in the Moluccas. By March 1580 Drake had reached Java. After another three months of sailing across the Indian Ocean, they rounded the Cape of Good Hope and headed up the coast of West Africa towards England.

Arriving in Plymouth near the end of September, Drake then sailed to the Palace of Greenwich (B9) on the

Statue of Sir Francis Drake -
Plymouth Hoe

Thames, arriving on 4 April 1581, when Queen Elizabeth gave a great banquet in his honour on board the ship and knighted him Sir Francis. The *Golden Hind* was laid up at Deptford as a national memorial to Drake's achievements. It eventually rotted away in the late 17th century. Drake was not only the first Englishman to circumnavigate the earth but also the first to found a colony on the western side of the North American continent.

When Mary Queen of Scots was executed at Fotheringhay Castle, Northamptonshire (B35) in February 1587, Philip II of Spain, aware that her death had robbed him of any chance of an alliance with the English throne, decided to invade England. Word of his plans was passed to the English and Drake led a fleet of ships into the Spanish port of Cadiz where he sank or captured about 30 ships, captured two forts and then plundered Spanish vessels laden with treasure just off the Azores. This expedition was known as the 'singeing of the King of Spain's beard'. The Spanish Armada finally set sail for England in July 1588. The English fleet of 190 ships was under the command of Lord Howard of Effingham and under the captaincies of Sir Francis Drake, Martin Frobisher and John Hawkins. The Armada was heavily defeated and only 55 ships of the once great fleet returned to Spanish shores.

Drake fell from the Queen's grace as his seafaring activities became less successful. He did, however, continue to play a public role both as Mayor of Plymouth and as a Member of Parliament. In 1595 another opportunity presented itself for him to take to the high seas in service of his Queen. It was rumoured that a treasure ship had been shipwrecked off Puerto Rico in the West Indies. Elizabeth recalled Drake to take command of an expedition together with his cousin, Sir John Hawkins, and between them they were given 27 ships.

Unfortunately, by the time they arrived at Puerto Rico, the Spanish were ready for them and ambushed them. Hawkins, by then an old man, died of dysentery. Drake also fell ill. Determined to die like a true soldier of England, he was fitted into his armour. After collapsing through sheer exhaustion, he died on 28 January

1596 and was buried at sea in a lead coffin in the waters off Panama.

Sir Francis Drake was for the most part associated with Plymouth. He was married in the church at St. Budeaux within the city. A statue of Drake, similar to one in the centre of Tavistock, stands on Plymouth Hoe looking out to sea. It was sculpted by Sir Edgar Boehm and unveiled in 1884.

In later years, Drake made his home at Buckland Abbey (A3), now a National Trust property, hidden in a secluded valley above the River Tavy. Originally, it was a Cistercian monastery and the house itself incorporates the 13th century abbey church. There are many items of memorabilia on show as well as displays featuring the history of Buckland. One of the items on display is the famous 'Drake's Drum'. It is emblazoned with his coat of arms and the legend goes that as he lay dying on board ship, he instructed that the drum be placed in St. Andrew's Church in Plymouth. He stated that if the drum were beaten in times of danger, he would return!

A faithful reconstruction of the *Golden Hind* is moored in South London at St. Mary Overie Dock, beside the Riverside Walk in Southwark (B10). With staff in period costume, this floating museum, in one of London's oldest docks, gives an authentic glimpse of seafaring life in Elizabethan times.

Martin Frobisher (1535-1594) was another seadog who ventured forth to explore the continent beyond the Atlantic and in 1576 set off with two ships in search of a north-west Passage. Unfortunately, one had to return just after they had reached Greenland, but Frobisher pushed on until he reached latitude 63° North where he approached what he thought were the straits of Asia. On his return to England, he brought with him some black mineral which was found to contain elements of gold. This led to the founding of the Cathay Company which soon attracted investors.

A second journey was made the following year with the purpose of retrieving further gold but little was actually extracted. On Frobisher's third journey in 1577, the intention had been to found a new colony – on the land mass now known as Baffin Island off the coast of Canada – and try to discover a passage to India. The expedition was, however, fraught with misfortune as Frobisher Bay was frozen. However, they did manage to gather ore to take back to England. As it turned out, the mineral proved valueless and the Cathay Company eventually went bankrupt.

In 1574 a petition was forwarded to Queen Elizabeth for permission for Sir Humphrey Gilbert (1539-83), a landowner from Devon, to proceed on a journey of exploration in an attempt to find a north-west Passage and discover new lands for the English crown. His home was Compton Castle (A8), a fortified manor house at Maridon near Paignton. The building, dating from the 14th century, sits in a lush valley and was the family home of the Gilberts. A stone courtyard is surrounded by towers and battlements and there is also a great hall, minstrels' gallery and spiral staircase. The property is maintained by the National Trust and open to the public.

It was four years before the Queen gave permission and granted Letters Patent to Humphrey Gilbert. These stated that settlers would have to stay in a new colony for at least ten years. They also prescribed he should 'take possession of all remote and barbarous lands unoccupied by any Christian Prince or people'. This was actually the first charter from England which 'authorised the settlement of new lands and to guarantee the legal and constitutional rights of the inhabitants'. Gilbert set sail with his fleet from Plymouth in November 1578 but they were met by heavy storms and, reluctantly, had to return to England. In 1583 Gilbert made another attempt, and in August of that year was able to claim Newfoundland for the English crown. However, he was not successful in persuading his men to settle in such a bleak place and decided to return home to England. Gilbert was distraught and drowned in a small boat whilst reading a copy of Sir Thomas More's *Utopia* (a book based on reports of an unexplored North American continent) during the homeward journey.

Sir Humphrey Gilbert was half-brother to Walter Raleigh (1552-1618), one of the most dashing and daring of Elizabeth's seafaring courtiers. He was not only known for his military achievements but also as a talented poet and historian. He was born at Hayes Barton, a tiny hamlet in South Devon, close to the village of East Budleigh (A10), once a town of wool dyers and smugglers. His birthplace has a substantial thatched roof and, though privately-owned, can clearly be viewed from the road. In the nearby church of All Saints in East Budleigh is the Raleigh pew with an inscription dated 1537. The pew-ends in this red sandstone church are unique in South Devon.

The nearby seaside town of Budleigh Salterton (A9) also has a connection with Raleigh as The Octagon was the home of Sir John G. Millais who painted 'The Boyhood of Raleigh' kept at London's Tate Britain Gallery on Millbank.

When Elizabeth had first been attracted to the tall, handsome Walter Raleigh, she presented him with land in Ireland, and on the death of Sir Humphrey Gilbert gave him permission to found new colonies for her in America. He took on the task of organising two trips to America in 1584 and 1585. As a preliminary, Raleigh fostered a small expedition to search for a site in April 1584 and they set out via the Canaries and West Indies and sailed northwards until they reached the island of Roanoke and re-named it Wyngandacoia. On hearing the report of this voyage, the English Queen was delighted and, according to popular belief, gave permission for the new land to be called Virginia in honour of herself. Some still argue that the name was derived from Wyngandacoia or even the local native American Indian chief, Wingina.

Over the winter of 1584 to 1585, Raleigh worked in earnest to organise the transportation and housing of his new colonists and they set out in April 1585 from Plymouth under the command of Sir Richard Grenville, Raleigh's cousin. They settled at Roanoke. After the initial success of these voyages, Walter Raleigh was knighted by his Queen. However, life proved to be hard at Roanoke and there was much fighting with the native American Indians. Food was short and conditions were unacceptable to many. By chance, Sir Francis Drake called in on his return from the West Indies and he was persuaded to take the settlers back to England.

Another group of colonists was sent out by Raleigh in 1587 headed by John White, an artist, who soon realised they had too few supplies. In consequence, they headed home and were then prevented from returning to Roanoke due to the war with Spain when all available English ships were on stand by. This prevented further attempts until 1606 when James I granted a charter to the Virginia Company of London.

In 1595, Raleigh had met and fallen for one of Queen Elizabeth's maids of honour at the English court. Elizabeth Throckmorton – better known as Bessie – came from an aristocratic Roman Catholic family in the Midlands who lived at Coughton Court (c4), near Alcester in Warwickshire. Raleigh and Bessie were clandestinely married when she was five months pregnant. Had they first sought the Queen's blessing for the marriage, Elizabeth might well have condoned it. On hearing the news she was furious and ordered them to the Tower of London. Eventually they were released and Raleigh tried hard to regain the Queen's favour by organising a voyage of exploration to Guiana on the northern coast of South America. It had always been believed that this was the location of the legendary El Dorado. On reaching the West Indies, they anchored off Trinidad and proceeded up the Orinoco River and into South American jungle. Like others before them, they did not find any legendary empire and returned to England empty-handed.

His reputation in tatters, Raleigh stayed for some time at the White Hart Inn in Salisbury (A12). The building is a Georgian fronted house, just off the High Street, quite close to the magnificent Salisbury Cathedral which boasts the tallest spire in England at 123 metres high. The cathedral was first consecrated in 1258 and in the south transept is the oldest clock in England. There are 13th century roof paintings and many elaborate tombs. Some of the memorials are to ancestors of Americans, in particular Sir Thomas Gorges of Massachusetts and the Brighams, from whom Robert Worth Brigham, US Ambassador, traced his descent. In the city which grew up around Cathedral Close are some interesting back streets with a medieval Poultry Cross where fowls were once sold, an Elizabethan Joiners Hall and the George Inn dating back to 1406.

Around the time of his marriage, Sir Walter Raleigh had been granted a 99-year lease on the 12th-century Sherborne Castle (A11), Dorset, and its deer park of over 1,000 acres (1.56 square kilometres). During the 1590s he built a magnificent mansion known as Sherborne Lodge, which forms the nucleus of the present house. It is commonly referred to as Sherborne Castle and is situated on the bank of the River Yeo. Though much of the original castle became a casualty of the Civil Wars and is now in ruins, the house remains. The gardens, designed by Capability Brown in the mid-18th century, include hanging terraces, orchards and a bowling green. There is also a stone seat in the gardens where Raleigh would sit to enjoy smoking his pipe of tobacco and, on one occasion, a servant is said to have doused him with ale when he thought his master was on fire! According to tradition, Sir Walter was the person who not only introduced tobacco and smoking into the country but also brought the potato to European shores. Smoking tobacco was a practice which King James I discouraged. He was convinced that smoking was bad for one's health and he issued a directive which must be considered as Britain's first anti-smoking campaign. His *Counterblaste to Tobacco* described smoking as 'a custom lothsome to the eye, hatefull to the nose, harmefull to the braine, dangerous to the lungs'. How close to the truth he really was!

Nearby Sherborne Abbey (A11) contains elements which date back to Saxon times when Sherborne was made the see of the Bishop of Wessex in 705 AD. The name of the ancient kingdom of Wessex was recently revived when Queen Elizabeth II created her youngest son, Edward, Earl of Wessex on his marriage to Sophie Rhys-Jones at St. George's Chapel, Windsor (B13), in July 1999.

After Queen Elizabeth's death at Richmond Palace (B11) on 24 March 1603, King James VI of Scotland was proclaimed the new monarch, James I. Raleigh became involved in a plot to depose him in favour of the Lady Arabella Stuart who was of royal lineage. She was the grand-daughter of the ambitious Bess, Countess of Shrewsbury who was born at Old Hardwick Hall, Derbyshire (D7) and was the builder of the new hall, completed in 1597, which was one of the finest Elizabethan mansions in the country. When the facts were exposed, Raleigh was imprisoned in the Tower and kept there for twelve years. During that time, his home and estate at Sherborne reverted to the Crown. Whilst in prison, Sir Walter completed the first volume of *The History of the World* which was published in 1614.

Eventually King James released him from the Tower in order that he might undertake another expedition to El Dorado. This proved disastrous and led to a battle with the Spaniards. For his failures, Raleigh was executed in the Old Palace Yard, Westminster, on 29 October 1618. Lady Raleigh lived until 1647 and it is understood that, wherever she went, she carried her husband's embalmed skull in a red leather bag. The actual burial place of Raleigh remains a mystery. It is thought that his body was buried at St. Margaret's Church, Westminster where, in 1882, American citizens placed a memorial window. According to a letter written by Lady Raleigh to her brother, his burial place was the Carew vault at the 14th century St. Mary's Church, Beddington (B8), situated west of Croydon in South London.

The reign of Queen Elizabeth I was one of the most successful of all English monarchs. There had been the discovery of new lands by explorers such as Frobisher, the Cabots, Drake and Raleigh, expansion in overseas trade, the sciences, religion and the arts. It had also been an era of dramatists and poets such as William Shakespeare, Christopher Marlowe, Francis Bacon and Ben Jonson. The musical world was enhanced by the work of composers William Byrd and Thomas Tallis, both of whom had been directors of music at the Chapel Royal.

Under the new monarch, James I, great changes were about to take place.

CHAPTER 3

The Beginning of a New Era

ONE OF THE MOST significant developments in the 16th century was the translation of the Bible into the English language by William Tyndale (1494-1536). (Martin Luther (1483-1546), Protestant leader of the German Reformation, had earlier translated the Bible into German.) This opened up new and wider possibilities for the ordinary person not educated in foreign languages such as Latin – the language of the Roman Catholic Church. It meant that anyone who was able to read could now study the Bible. People were able to meet together to read, worship and discuss their thoughts and findings as well as listen to the words of preachers. From these small beginnings, the tradition of family prayers was established, more in keeping with the simplicity of the New Testament tradition. Soon, people began to form their own religious views rather than accepting, without question, the rigid doctrines of the Established Church. Despite the break from the Roman Catholic Church and the establishment of a Protestant Church by Henry VIII in 1534, a growing number of Protestant worshippers felt that it had not gone far enough. This led to the start of the Puritan movement and it gained support throughout the reign of Elizabeth I but, in the main, it had been suppressed.

Those who wanted further radical reform became known as 'Separatists'. By and large, this religious unrest took hold in country parishes rather than in the larger centres which were more under the control and influence of the clergy and the bishops.

When James VI of Scotland was proclaimed James I in 1603, the Separatists and other Puritan groups hoped they would be granted wider religious freedom. After all, he had been brought up in the Protestant faith. An approach was therefore made to the new monarch even before he reached London from Scotland. In their petition to the King, these groups requested that changes be

adopted by the Established Church such as less music, shorter services and less emphasis on ceremonial dress. Initially, King James
did not dismiss the ideas but actually thought it would give him an
opportunity to help re-unite the factions of the Established
Church. Naturally, the bishops and those in the higher echelons of
the Church of England, mainly made up of Conformists, were violently opposed to any form of compromise.

Early in 1604, the King called the Hampton Court Conference
(B12) to hear both sides of the argument. Eventually, he came
down on the side of the bishops and other traditionalists despite
pleas for more freedom of worship by Nonconformists. He finally
declared, much to their despair, 'I will make them conform themselves, or I will harry them out of the land!' As a result of this
edict, nearly 90 clerics were stripped of their livings and the persecution of groups such as the Separatists began in earnest.

There were initially two groups of active religious dissenters,
one centred on the town of Gainsborough (D18) in Lincolnshire
and the other on the tiny village of Babworth (D13), situated on
the borders of Yorkshire, Nottinghamshire and Lincolnshire.

Gainsborough, the St. Ogg's in George Eliot's novel, *The Mill
on the Floss*, stands on the banks of the River Trent. Ashcroft
Mill, which stood near the bridge over the river, was the mill on
which the book was based. The oldest building in the town is a
manor house in Lord Street, with oak timber framing, a stone
tower with an oriel window, and towers of small bricks, the whole
forming three sides of a quadrangle. This is known as
Gainsborough Old Hall and was built around 1460 by Sir Thomas
Burgh. It is one of the largest medieval buildings in England and
is open to the public. Richard III stayed there in 1484 and later
visitors include Henry VIII and his sixth wife, Catherine Parr. It is
closely associated with the early Separatists. John Wesley, founder
of The Methodist Church, preached there on several occasions.

In 1602, a Separatist named John Smyth from Lincoln (D10)
was dismissed by his Bishop for expressing radical views on
Puritanism and preaching 'strange doctrines' to his congregation.
Smyth had studied at Cambridge (B33) and was a Fellow of

Christ's College. Other early Separatists were also educated at the University which had become a hotbed of Nonconformism.

At the time when the Separatists were first starting to form their Church, the Hall at Gainsborough was inhabited by a family called Hickman which had a strong Puritan background. William Hickman and his mother, Rose, were both religious exiles and had great sympathy with the Separatists. Rose Hickman befriended John Smyth after his dismissal from Lincoln and offered him shelter at the Hall which they allowed to be used for meetings of the Separatist Church. Smyth became pastor of the new church and numbers in his congregation rapidly increased.

Babworth is a few miles south-west of Gainsborough and about two miles west of the town of Retford. Just opposite the junction of the A620 with the B6420 west of Retford (D13) is a narrow lane leading to isolated woodland. Hidden from view at the end of the track is the Parish Church of All Saints. It is generally accepted that it was here that the Pilgrim movement was born.

The rector at Babworth was Richard Clyfton who had arrived there in 1586. He was born at Normanton (C12) near Derby in 1553 and was one of a large family. He went to Cambridge University where he soon fell under the spell of Nonconformist preachers who left a marked impression upon the young undergraduate. He inherited from them a desire for religious liberty and expression plus freedom of conscience. Although he became an ordained clergyman of the Church of England, his message to his congregation was always simple. He would explain the Word of God in easy language, without pomp and ceremony, so that his flock were able to understand his teachings. Soon after arriving at Babworth, Clyfton married Anne Stuffen of nearby Warsop (D8) with whom he had six children. He proved to be a thoughtful and charismatic rector who quickly endeared himself to his congregation. It was not long before people in neighbouring villages were drawn to the preachings of Richard Clyfton and numbers attending his services began to increase.

Two members of his congregation were William Brewster of Scrooby (D16), Nottinghamshire, and William Bradford of

Austerfield (D17), just across the boundary with Yorkshire. Brewster is regarded by many as the real founder of the Pilgrim movement. A most kindly and learned man, he was to mastermind the whole Mayflower adventure to the New World in 1620.

Brewster and Bradford, along with others from surrounding villages, walked to the Parish Church of All Saints at Babworth along a track which is now known as 'Pilgrim's Way'. (In 1950, a silver chalice was discovered under the floor of the church by workmen. It is thought it might have been hidden for safety during the time of the Civil Wars. The chalice was made in 1593 during Clyfton's ministry and used for Holy Communion.) The church was built in 1290 but has undergone several restorations. A number of commemorative items relating to the Pilgrim Fathers can be seen in the building. These include several plaques, a model of the *Mayflower* made from matchsticks and a painting of the Babworth congregation on their way to church painted by a former inmate of the nearby Ranby prison.

The Church authorities got wind of Richard Clyfton's style of preaching and the way in which he was conducting services. They soon started to harass him. Eventually, in 1605, he was accused

All Saints' Church, Babworth, Nottinghamshire

before the Chancery Court of being a Nonconformist in his role as parson at Babworth Church. He was accused of failing to use the Book of Common Prayer, not using the sign of the Cross during baptismal ceremonies, and failing to wear his cap and surplice during church services. The outcome was that he was deprived of his living at Babworth.

Clyfton was invited to move to Scrooby Manor House (D16) to stay with William Brewster and, together with Bradford and a few others, started to attend John Smyth's services at Gainsborough. In 1604, John Smyth was reported for preaching in Gainsborough and tried two years later at the Royal Court. He fled with some of his followers to Amsterdam (E1) to join a group of Separatists led by Francis Johnson and Henry Ainsworth, both from London. Shortly afterwards, William Brewster and William Bradford set up their own Separatist group at Scrooby Manor and re-commenced their services in the privacy of Brewster's home.

Scrooby Manor had a proud history. The village of Scrooby was set by the Great North Road and had long been an important staging post. A settlement had existed in 958 AD when King Edgar granted lands to the Archbishop of York. It is thought that the Manor House, or Archbishop's Palace, was probably built in the 12th century, to accommodate him during his journeyings around the diocese. It was a substantial building with 40 rooms and a private chapel. It is known that King John stayed there in 1207. Margaret Tudor, elder sister of Henry VIII, stopped off on her way to Scotland to marry James IV.

Cardinal Wolsey also stayed during the summer of 1530 en route to stand trial in London for high treason. He was moved to Sheffield Manor (D5) in November, where he was taken ill. He then journeyed southwards but, fortunately for him, died at Leicester Abbey (C11) before reaching London and what would almost certainly have been death by the executioner's axe. Eleven years later, King Henry VIII held a privy council at Scrooby. By the time of the Separatist meetings in the early 17th century, the property was most probably in decline. Today, only one wing of the once magnificent mansion remains and this is used as a farmhouse, Manor Farm. It is private property but there is a viewpoint 100 metres along Station Road from which the house and adjoining land can be seen. The Pilgrim links with the building are commemorated in wall plaques.

The parish church at Scrooby is dedicated to St. Wilfrid (634-707 AD) Archbishop of York. He was educated at the monastery of Lindisfarne and it was at the Synod of Whitby (D26) in 664 AD that he was mainly responsible for the decision to Romanise the Church's calendar. The first reference to a church at Scrooby occurs in the late 12th century. Much rebuilding took place in the 14th century when the distinctive tower with its octagonal base was added. It was further enlarged in the 16th century when a south aisle and porch were built. It was here that the Brewster family worshipped and the reputed Brewster pew can still be viewed with its ornate carvings. In 1864, the church underwent a major restoration and refurbishment scheme, after which certain items were sent to America including a medieval font which was transported to the Wellington Avenue United Church of Christ in Chicago in 1881. A pew back was donated to Pilgrim Hall Museum in Plymouth, Massachusetts. As Scrooby church registers only date from 1695, it is impossible to prove whether William Brewster was baptised there.

The village of Scrooby is a quiet haven yet just a short distance from the A638 trunk road on which is situated the Pilgrim Fathers Inn. The hostelry dates from the 18th century and only acquired its name in 1969 for commemorative purposes. Scrooby is a pretty village with some picturesque corners, such as Monks Mill situated on the old course of the River Ryton, used by the Separatists as an escape route to the east coast.

William Bradford was born at Austerfield in Yorkshire, close to the border with Nottinghamshire and only five kilometres from Scrooby. Church records reveal that he was baptised on 19 March 1589 at the Church of St. Helena (D17), a short distance from his home. According to tradition, this was the Manor House, a lovely dark-timbered building along the A614 road to Thorne. It is clearly visible from the roadway but is privately owned. In its cellars some of the Separatists hid whilst they were being hunted by Church authorities.

Although there was probably an earlier wooden building on the site, The Church of St. Helena was built soon after the Norman conquest about the year 1080 by John de Builli whose daughter gave it to the Priory of Blyth (D15). Much of the original stonework survives from that period though it is thought the building was enlarged in the 13th century. A further restoration was carried out in the late 19th century. At the time, some fine Norman pillars were discovered which had hitherto been concealed within a wall. The church is dedicated to St. Helena, mother of the Emperor Constantine, who made Christianity the religion of the Roman Empire.

The Bradfords were a farming family and William was an orphan brought up by his uncles. By the time he was twelve, he had started to study the Bible and it was not long before he began to journey to Gainsborough to listen to the Reverend John Smyth and later to Babworth to learn more of the teachings of Richard Clyfton. He was seventeen when he went to live at Scrooby with William Brewster. It was the start of a life-long association.

During the Elizabethan era, Brewster's father, William Snr, was appointed Bailiff of the Manor of Scrooby in 1575, responsible to the Archbishop for the administration of his Scrooby estate. Thirteen years later he was given an additional position of 'Master of the Queen's Postes' – appointed by the Government to act as representative to forward correspondence, accommodate officials and provide them with lodging on their travels between London and Scotland along the Great North Road.

William Jnr. was sent to Peterhouse College, Cambridge, in 1580 and became influenced by the radical thinkers in religious matters. He went to work for William Davison, a Secretary of State who, in 1585, was Queen Elizabeth I's representative to the Netherlands. Young William Brewster joined him there. However, Davison fell from favour just over a year later. He had been ordered by Queen Elizabeth to draw up the death warrant of Mary Queen of Scots. After the execution of Mary, Elizabeth blamed him for being too hasty in producing the document and not only confiscated his estates but also condemned him to the Tower of London.

The change in his master's circumstances resulted in William Jnr. returning to Scrooby. His father died in 1590 and, eventually, William was appointed to his father's positions. His pay was twenty pence per day which was later raised to two shillings to which could be added additional costs for entertaining in his home and also the letting out of properties to private travellers up and down the Great North Road.

For the visitor who is seeking to explore this area of Nottinghamshire, Lincolnshire and South Yorkshire, popularly known as Pilgrim Father Country in local tourist brochures, a good starting point could be the Worksop Museum (D14) with its excellent 'Pilgrim Fathers Story and Exhibition'. This is a comprehensive display about the early days of the Separatist movement, the Pilgrim Fathers, and the locations with which they were associated in that part of Middle England. Worksop has for years been known as the 'Gateway to the Dukeries' due to its close proximity to the ducal estates of Clumber, Thoresby, Welbeck and Worksop Manor and just a short drive away from Sherwood Forest of Robin Hood fame near Edwinstowe (D9). From here, a short walk can be made to see the Major Oak, reputedly where the legendary hero once hid from the Sheriff of Nottingham's men. The tree has a girth of 33 feet (10 metres). In Edwinstowe church is a stone altar where Robin Hood is said to have married Maid Marion. The nearby town of Retford is also a good centre for touring the various Pilgrim and Robin Hood sites, having a range of historic buildings, pedestrianised streets, a large market square, a museum and ancient churches.

Another Separatist who played an important role in the life of early Nonconformists was John Robinson who was born in the village of Sturton-le-Steeple (D12), Nottinghamshire, in 1578. John Smyth was also born there. The lofty tower of the Church of St. Peter and St. Paul, topped by twelve pinnacles, is the only part to have escaped a fire in 1901. Restoration of the church took place based on the old design and incorporated original building material. It is thought that the present chancel was probably the original Norman church. Until the middle of the 20th century, the windmill and church tower of Sturton-le-Steeple were the two out-standing landmarks in the area. Today, with the encroachment of urbanisation onto a rural landscape, they are dwarfed by the cool-ing towers of nearby power stations at West Burton and Cottam.

Like Smyth, Clyfton and Brewster, John Robinson was edu-cated at Cambridge and entered Corpus Christi College in 1592, becoming a fellow in 1597. He excelled in theology and was greatly influenced at Cambridge by the charismatic preachers, Thomas Cartwright and Robert 'Troublechurch' Browne, and was drawn towards the Separatist movement. He was forced to resign his fel-lowship when he married his childhood sweetheart, Bridget White, who came from the same village of Sturton-le-Steeple though they were married at St. Mary's Church, Greasley (C14) in Nottinghamshire, near to Bridget's home at Beauvale Priory.

It is possible to follow in the footsteps of some of the early Separatists around the city of Cambridge. John Smyth's College – Christ's – was founded in 1437 by the Reverend William Byngham and re-instituted in 1505 by Lady Margaret Beaufort, mother of Henry VII. First Court was built at this time, but rebuilt in the 18th century. John Milton, a Puritan and famed for his epic poem 'Paradise Lost' (1667), wrote his earliest works while a student at Christ's College. William Brewster's College – Peterhouse – was founded in two houses in 1284 by Hugh Balsam, Bishop of Ely, and a hall was built two years later. This is the only building to survive from the 13th century, though it underwent extensive restoration when the interior was decorated by William Morris. Nearby Corpus Christi College, where John Robinson studied, includes the best surviving early medieval college court in Cambridge. Building of Old Court commenced in 1352 but New Court was not added until the early 19th century. The college is unique among Oxford (A20) and Cambridge colleges in having been founded by townsfolk. Both Universities of Cambridge and Oxford were originally for members of the Anglican Church. The first university to be built for Nonconformists and other faiths was University College in London.

The visitor to Cambridge should try and see the interior of the magnificent King's College Chapel and its beautiful fan vaulting built between 1512-15. The best time to stroll around the city sites and college grounds, many of which are open to the public, is an early summer evening when the bustle of traffic and tourists have left and one can wander at ease in the quadrangles and backstreets. It is then that one perhaps feels a real sense of history.

After leaving Cambridge, John Robinson was appointed parson at the parish church in Mundham (B26), Norfolk, where he was soon in trouble with church authorities for his radical form of preaching. He was deprived of his living and moved to St. Andrew's Church in Norwich (B28) where there was more sympathy for his form of worship. Yet he was still persecuted for his beliefs and, soon afterwards, he gravitated towards Scrooby to join William Brewster. On the formation of the Separatist Church at Scrooby, Robinson became the teacher, Clyfton, the pastor, and Brewster, an elder. The group continued with their daily prayer, study of the Bible and clandestine services without any undue interference. However, there was trouble on the horizon.

CHAPTER 4

Storm Clouds Gather

AFTER THE HAMPTON COURT Conference in 1604 new decrees were put into operation and these included a ban on any private religious meeting. The Separatists at Scrooby found this particularly frustrating and the threat of exposure to the Church authorities was always there. Punishment for anyone who did not conform with the decrees was severe. Details of the Scrooby meetings soon reached the ears of the Archbishop of York and the Bishop of Lincoln who were already well aware of Clyfton and his associates through their earlier defiance of Church rules and ritual. In any punishment meted out to them, they should be used as an example to other dissenters. The persecution began.

According to the journal of William Bradford, '.... some were taken up and clapt in prison .... others had their houses beset and watched day and night .... and most were fain to fly and leave their houses and habitations and their means of livelihood'. William Brewster was summoned to appear before the authorities at York (D23) and fined twenty pounds for disobedience. The Separatists' behaviour was considered disloyal to the Crown and, as a result, there was considerable persecution of anyone found to be defying the regulations of the Established Church. The Scrooby group lived in fear of reprisals and, during this period, Brewster's wife, Mary, gave birth to a baby girl whom they christened Fear. (They already had a son, Jonathan, and a daughter, Patience.) The outlook for the Separatists was not good. Some radical steps would have to be taken if they were to be able to continue in their chosen form of worship. There was really only one solution open to them. They must emigrate to a country which would be more sympathetic to their cause – the Netherlands.

In theory, this sounded a good idea, but in practice there were so many things to be considered. For a start, there were families and the cost of transportation to Holland. The exodus of Separatists would have to take place in secret to avoid discovery. Even as far back as the reign of Richard II, a parliamentary statute prohibited emigration without a licence. For anyone not complying with this edict, the penalty was imprisonment. A decision to proceed was therefore not taken lightly as it would place everyone in grave danger. Yet the Separatists had great faith and were convinced that the good Lord would eventually 'deliver them into their own Promised Land'. They knew that John Smyth and some of his congregation from Gainsborough, suffering similar persecution, had already taken the decision and were settled in Amsterdam (E1).

John Robinson and William Brewster agreed that the Scrooby group should depart for Holland and Brewster made arrangements to charter a boat from Boston (B36) in Lincolnshire to convey them across the North Sea. In the meantime, funds had to be raised by selling their homes and most of their belongings. Even in a small village such as Scrooby, they had to be specially vigilant as there were local people who readily would have betrayed the Separatists because of the rich rewards being offered for the exposure of any illegal emigrants. Brewster resigned his office as 'Master of the King's Postes' at Scrooby in September 1607 which, in itself, must have made some suspicious.

In the following month, a group of about 60 people, led by Brewster, and including the eighteen-year-old William Bradford, travelled overland, in small groups, to the port of Boston to await a passage across the North Sea. Brewster had come to an arrangement with a ship's captain after much bargaining and having had to agree an extortionate sum as the price of the passage. As they reached their point of departure, men, women and children must have been cold, frightened and anxious about what might lie in store for them. They boarded the vessel at Scotia Creek (B37), near Fishtoft, a deserted wind-swept place beyond Boston and closer to the open sea. Once they were all on board and below deck, the captain fastened them in, even before they had had the time to store their belongings. He and his crew then proceeded to pillage the cargo and robbed the passengers of all their money and valuables. The wily captain then sent a message to the port's authorities informing them of his capture of illegal emigrants. It was not long before the frightened Separatists were arrested by the 'catchpoles' (constables or bailiffs).

A granite obelisk now marks the spot at Scotia Creek where the Pilgrim Fathers tried to embark. They were conducted back up river in open boats to Boston and thrown into cells at the Guildhall to await trial. Surprisingly enough, the magistrates were reasonably sympathetic to their cause as the town was mainly Nonconformist. However, they were unable to deal wholly with the Separatists as it was up to the ecclesiastical authorities to decide their fate. In the main, the majority of Separatists were imprisoned for a month and then sent back to their own parishes, including William Bradford because of his young age. However, seven were retained including John Robinson, Richard Clyfton and William Brewster to await trial at the assizes to be held in Lincoln Castle (D10). Eventually, after much local support and pressure, the prisoners were released. Like the rest of their flock, they made their way back to Scrooby and adjoining parishes, completely penniless, to decide on their plans for the future.

Boston is a fine old market town with many historical links, situated on the quiet but fast flowing River Witham. It has been a port for hundreds of years and traded mainly with Flanders. The gradual silting up of the estuary over the years has prevented larger ships reaching the docks. The town is dominated by the tower of the historic Church of St. Botolph, better known as Boston Stump, a landmark which can be seen from over 60 kilometres across the flatlands of Lincolnshire and from the North Sea. It has a magnificent medieval lantern tower and would have been known to the Pilgrims as well as many sailors out at sea when the lantern light was lit each evening. It is also fondly known as a 'calendar' church in that it can boast 365 steps to the top of the lantern, 12 supporting pillars to the roof, 7 doors and 52 windows (now 51 as one has been removed to America).

St. Botolph's has several fine tombs and monumental brasses

and a 17th century pulpit. For the hardy, it is well worth the climb to the top of the tower as the panorama is magnificent, embracing one third of the county. It is particularly colourful in springtime when the surrounding area is a patchwork of blazing colours with the many hectares of flowers which are grown in this eastern part of England. The church tower contains a peal of ten bells and a carillon of fifteen bells. At the west end of the south aisle is a chapel restored in 1857 by the people of Boston (F25) Massachusetts in memory of the Reverend John Cotton, who held a living in the town between 1612 and 1633. He was educated at Derby Free Grammar School (C12) before taking up the priesthood. He resigned his post at St. Botolph's owing to his Nonconformist views and emigrated to Trimountain (now Boston, Massachusetts) where he became first minister of the Christian Church in 1633. He died in 1652. The pulpit of St. Botolph's dates from 1612, the year in which John Cotton became vicar in Boston, but the Cotton Chapel actually dates from the mid-1800s.

Boston Guildhall, where some of the Pilgrims were imprisoned, is a fine brick structure which dates from 1450. It had once been the hall of St. Mary's Guild, founded in 1260, the earliest and wealthiest of fifteen religious guilds in Boston. The building continued to be used by the local corporation for dining and meetings until 1864 when these activities were transferred to the Assembly Rooms. The property was restored in 1911 and is now used as a borough museum. It contains a courtroom where some of the Separatists were tried, two fine fireplaces and, in the west window, some ancient stained glass. Perhaps of most interest and importance are the cells on the ground floor in which the Separatists were imprisoned.

Guildhall, Boston, Lincolnshire

Alongside the Guildhall is a Georgian building, Fydell House, which was built in 1726 by William Fydell, three times Mayor of Boston. It contains interesting panelling and one of the finest carved staircases of the period in the country. It also has an American Room which was opened by the then American Ambassador to Britain, the Hon. Joseph P. Kennedy (father of President John F. Kennedy) in July 1938, and dedicated to the use of visitors from Boston's American namesake in Massachusetts.

By the spring of 1608 the Separatists were ready to make a second attempt to leave England for Holland. William Bradford and one or two others had managed to board a ship and had arrived safely in Holland after a rough voyage. For the main party, William Brewster made contact with a Dutch ship owner in Hull (D22) who agreed to convey the group from a deserted stretch of beach on the Lincolnshire side of the Humber estuary, On this occasion, at dead of night, the women, children and belongings were conveyed in small boats from Scrooby along Ryton Water to Bawtry (D17) and then down the Idle and Trent. They met up with their menfolk who had walked the distance of 64 kilometres overland at an agreed meeting point – Killingholme Creek (D21). Today, it is the site of the busy port of Immingham Dock. The final departure of the Scrooby Separatists to Holland is marked by a monument opposite the parish church in Immingham. It was moved to its present position in 1970 from Immingham Dock and is made of stone brought from the shore of Plymouth, Massachusetts.

After their earlier experiences in Boston, the Pilgrims must have been doubly terrified, especially as there were several children and young infants in the group. Any sound could have alerted possible informers to their activities. By the time the Dutch ship finally appeared, many women and children were suffering from cold and exposure. The menfolk were first to clamber on board in case there was any re-occurrence of the Boston incident. Unfortunately, the ship ran aground on mud flats and they had to wait for the rising tide. Then disaster happened! A group of armed catchpoles appeared on the shore. On spotting them, the ship's captain managed to set sail and steered a course down the River

Humber. The menfolk on board could only look on in despair as they saw their wives and children in the hands of the catchpoles, disappearing into the distance as the ship headed midstream in driving rain.

The North Sea crossing was not easy. The Dutch ship ran into a violent storm which carried it off course as far as Norway before they were finally able to head for Amsterdam.

There was little to be done with the terrified wives and children left stranded on the shore at Killingholme. After interrogation by the authorities, and with no homes to return to, they were eventually released. Not all the men had crossed to Holland. William Brewster and the two pastors, John Robinson and Richard Clyfton, had stayed behind to arrange matters and ensure the safe passage of every member of the Scrooby group who wished to make the journey. It was thus easier to arrange for the women and children to join those who had already gone to Amsterdam. Eventually, by August 1608, all the Separatists had arrived in Holland. They had become Pilgrims in another land. They had escaped England, the Anglican Church authorities, and the edicts of King James.

CHAPTER 5

Holland

17TH CENTURY AMSTERDAM was a bustling seaport, as indeed it still is today. This was the time and country of Rembrandt, Frans Hals, Jan van Goyen and other Dutch painters. Amsterdam has a unique setting on the south side of the IJsselmeer (formerly the Zuiderzee). With its vast network of picturesque canals, crossed by more than 800 bridges and lined with attractive old merchants' houses and museums, the city is a mecca for visitors who come to sample its liberal attitude toward free-thinking people. The 17th century must have been no exception.

The Scrooby group of Separatists would soon have felt at home in Amsterdam as they were greeted by two other exiled communities. There was John Smyth's group from Gainsborough with whom some of them were already acquainted. A second body, named the Ancient Brethren, an early band of Nonconformists, was led by Robert Browne and Francis Johnson of London. The Ancient Brethren came from various parts of England and had already settled in a suitable meeting house in Amsterdam situated in a narrow street still known as Brownist's Alley (Bruinistengange). The time of the Pilgrims in Amsterdam is commemorated in the Begijnhof Chapel, the city's English Reformed Church where there is a series of plaques and a stained glass window.

For some months life ran smoothly as people settled into their new way of life, but after a year the community became a little unsettled. Disagreements began to arise between the three groups about the ways in which each was conducting its affairs. John Smyth was the first to break away to form a second English Church in exile. It was not long before the Scrooby group did likewise. Some returned to England disillusioned.

One of the reasons why the Pilgrims did not settle in Amsterdam was the behaviour of Dutch children who were allowed a great deal of self-expression. The contrast with the sober and strict upbringing of the Pilgrim children was too great, and they were picking up bad habits. There was little integration with the Ancient Brethren who, in the main, were not as disciplined as the Scrooby brethren. There was even talk of scandalous behaviour amongst some of their members. The Scrooby group began to look elsewhere for a place which might be less disturbing and perhaps more tolerant of their lifestyle. Pastor Richard Clyfton decided to stay on in Amsterdam. He died there on 20 May 1616. His grave is in the old South Church and a street in Plymouth (F19), Massachusetts was later named after him.

On the recommendation of Pastor John Robinson, the Pilgrims chose the university town of Leiden (E2) as their new home. A letter was duly written to the Burgomasters requesting permission for the Pilgrims to settle there. This was granted on 12 February 1609 and the Pilgrims were accepted as residents of the city. The official acceptance stated 'that Leiden refuses no honest people free entry to come live in the city, as long as they behave honestly and obey all the laws and ordinances, and under those conditions the applicants' arrival here would be pleasing and welcome'.

Leiden was then Holland's second largest city and an English Puritan congregation had been in existence there since 1607 but

A windmill near Leiden

without its own minister. It formed part of the Reformed Church along with the French-speaking Walloon (Calvinist) congregation and the German and Dutch Reformed Churches. Two years later, when members of the English Reformed Church could not agree with the doctrines of the Separatists, the former petitioned for their own minister. Consequently, the Reverend Robert Dury became their pastor.

John Robinson, William Brewster, William Bradford and about 100 followers moved to Leiden which became their home for nearly twelve years.

With origins in Roman times, Leiden developed in the 12th century on the spot where the Rhine divides into three main streams – the Vliet, the Mare and Leede. Forty-five kilometres south of Amsterdam, Leiden was the birthplace of the painter Rembrandt (1606-1669) who spent 28 years of his life there. It was also the place where Clusius brought the first Dutch tulips into flower.

During the 16th and 17th centuries Leiden became prosperous and famous for cloth manufacture. In the Eighty Years War between Spain and the Netherlands (1568-1648), Leiden had played a significant role as it was the object of a major siege at the hands of the Spanish. The city's deliverance by the breaching of dikes to flood out their invaders has become a legend in Dutch history books. As a token of gratitude for its steadfastness, William of Orange offered the city a university, now the oldest and most important in the Netherlands. Founded in 1575, it soon attracted the great thinkers and scientists of the 16th and 17th centuries.

Today Leiden is handsome and well-preserved, and as you wander along picturesque canals, you see many monumental buildings, a hilltop castle, grand Gothic churches, almshouses and squares, all oases of peace and quiet. During term time, the streets are crowded with students cycling between lectures and packing the bookshops and cafès. The main street, the Breestraat, is a former Roman road. Many of the Pilgrims registered their marriages at the Town Hall. Civil marriage registration was one of several Dutch ideas they were later to introduce to America.

Whilst in Leiden, the visitor should take time to visit the Leiden American Pilgrim Museum located at Beschuitsteeg 9 in the city centre. Although small in size, it has a wealth of Pilgrim memorabilia, rare engravings and maps covering the time of the Separatists both in Holland and the New World.

One of the first priorities of the Pilgrims was to find employment. Several of the men were tradesmen so found it easier to get work while others had to be content with taking what work was available and some were fortunate in obtaining jobs, both skilled and unskilled, in the thriving cloth industry. It was not long before the group began to feel more settled after the problems they had experienced in Amsterdam.

With William Brewster's academic background, he became a tutor of English, teaching Dutch students. Brewster already had contacts in the city. He had been to Holland some years earlier and visited Leiden. His home was in a side-alley off Pieterskerkchoorsteeg, where, halfway down, the visitor can see the house in which the printing works, the Pilgrim Press, was first established. This alley was formerly known as the Stincksteeg (Stink Alley) but was later named William Brewstersteeg. A plaque, placed there by the Society of Mayflower Descendants, commemorates the Pilgrim links. Higher up the Pieterskerkchoorsteeg is the Walloon Church with its little steeple. This was formerly the Catharina Hospital.

John Robinson lived on the Kloksteeg (Bell Alley) and his house, Groene Port (Green Door), still stands opposite the Pieterskerk (St. Peter's Church), a large brick building, the oldest church in the city, dating from 1428. It contains a choir screen with a Renaissance frieze and a pulpit from 1532 beside a magnificent organ from 1637. Rembrandt's parents are buried there, as are the painter, Jan Steen, many Leiden university professors and Pastor John Robinson. There is a memorial tablet to him in the south-west corner together with other information about the Pilgrim Fathers including a family tree tracing the genealogy of former US Presidents Franklin Delano Roosevelt and George Bush from the Pilgrim Fathers.

By 1611 John Robinson was apparently concerned that many of his flock were scattered throughout the city and lacked co-ordination. He discussed this with his Elders to see what could be done. About this time the building called the Groene Port was put up for sale which was not only suitable for a family but also had a large room where meetings could be held. With financial assistance from some of his colleagues in the Separatist Church, Robinson was able to raise a deposit on the premises. The present inner courtyard and garden of the almshouse date from 1683, replacing Robinson's house.

Two houses away was the home of Thomas Brewer from Kent. He provided finance to set up the printing business for the Leiden Pilgrims. This furthered the Nonconformists' cause and enabled them to send their own translation of the Ten Commandments and other items of literature back to England. The master printer was John Reynolds and he was assisted by Edward Winslow (later Governor of New Plymouth). Winslow was travelling in Holland when he came across the Exile Church of Leiden in 1617, and he remained there, staying with John Robinson. In the following year Robinson officiated at the marriage of Edward Winslow to Elizabeth Barker.

Edward Winslow was born on 18 October 1595, the eldest of eight children. He came from a family of some standing in the little spa town of Droitwich (c5) in Worcestershire, though his grandfather, Kenelm, had a farmhouse at Kempsey (c1) near Worcester. St. Peter's Church, on the edge of Droitwich, is a lovely old building of red sandstone and dates back to Saxon times though little from that period survives. It was here that Edward was baptised on 20 October 1595 (a bronze plaque on the north wall of the nave commemorates the event). He was educated at Kings School in Worcester (c2) and became a printer in London. Droitwich has, since Roman times, been famous for its salt, in particular for its Brine Baths, Britain's only inland swimming pool with salt-water (only the Dead Sea has water as salty). The Brine Baths are situated in the compact and attractive centre of Droitwich which has many timber-framed buildings, a curiosity in themselves as they lean at peculiar angles due to ancient land settlement.

Edward Winslow and the Pilgrim movement are also commemorated at St. Bride's Church off Fleet Street, close to Ludgate Circus in the City of London. Edward's parents were married in the church and there is a stained glass window depicting the family connection with the Pilgrim Fathers. The original church was burned down in the Great Fire of London in 1666.

The Separatists were joined in Leiden by another man, Captain Miles Standish, who would prove to be a key figure in the movement of Pilgrims and Merchant Adventurers to the New World. Born in 1584, as a youth he had fought against Spain in the Netherlands where he acquired skills as a soldier with English troops sent by Queen Elizabeth to support the Dutch army. He was wounded in 1602 at the Siege of Ostend and nursed in the Catherina Hospital in Leiden. Standish was reputed to have a fiery temper and, due to his short stature, was nicknamed Captain Shrimp. He stayed on in Holland after truce was announced with Spain. The place of his birth is a subject of debate. There were various branches of the Standish family who had homes at Ellenbane on the Isle of Man and at Standish Hall, Standish, Ormskirk and Duxbury Hall, all in Lancashire. According to tradition, he was baptised at St. Lawrence's Church in Chorley (D4) which has a Standish Chapel and memorials to the family. Yet his name does not appear in parish registers covering the period of his birth. There is also a Standish Chapel in St. Wilfrid's Parish Church in the little town of Standish (D3).

Captain Standish first became acquainted with William Bradford, John Robinson and other Separatists in Leiden. He became invaluable to the Pilgrims both from a military point of view and for his organisational skills.

During the course of the next few years, several of the Pilgrims married and children were born. The group was joined by others from England such as John and Isaac Allerton, Jonathan Brewster – son of William, Edward Jessop, Moses Fletcher, William White, Thomas Blossom and Samuel Fuller.

* * *

In 1602 Captain Bartholomew Gosnold, of Grundisburgh

(B24), Suffolk, one of Raleigh's sea captains, set sail from Falmouth (A1) harbour in Cornwall on the *Concord*. His commission was to seek a new and shorter route to Virginia, a task he completed in seven weeks, and to explore the possibilities for emigration. From Virginia he continued along the New England coastline up to Maine and discovered and named both Martha's Vineyard (F6) and Cape Cod where he saw an extraordinary number of cod. Gosnold sailed southwards from Cape Cod until he reached Buzzard's Bay (F8), which he renamed Gosnold's Hope. He built a storehouse on a nearby island and named the settlement Elizabeth. The experience had a great influence on him and he returned to England, eager to further his vision, and soon set about raising support for a colonial venture.

In December 1606 three ships – the *Discovery* captained by John Ratcliffe, the *Susan Constant* commanded by Christopher Newport, and *Godspeed* captained by Gosnold himself, set out from Blackwall on the River Thames on a venture which led to the first permanent settlement of the English in America. The colony was governed by six members of a council, including Gosnold and Ratcliffe. A few months after arriving, Gosnold's death from swamp fever was a serious blow to the colony.

One person who had been infected by Gosnold's enthusiasm was Captain John Smith, a seasoned adventurer who was born at Willoughby (D11) near Alford in Lincolnshire. He was baptised at St. Helene's Church which has a number of fine stained glass windows which depict scenes from his life. As a youth, he ran away to sea to escape a mundane apprenticeship. Smith was involved in the establishment of the Jamestown colony in 1607. He was elected President of Virginia the following year. A serious fire in 1607 destroyed all the buildings in Jamestown but Smith managed to rally the colony through the winter. Within three months, half the colonists had died of disease and the rest faced starvation and they turned to John Smith to seek help and supplies from the Indians. He duly set out and travelled 50 miles (80 kilometres) up the James River before he was captured by warriors of the Powhatan tribe. He might well have been slain there and then but for his quick thinking in showing and describing his compass. He was escorted to the Indian settlement where he was sentenced to death.

When he was about to be killed, the chief's fourteen-year-old daughter, Princess Pocahontas, flung herself across Smith's body to protect him, pleading for his life. As a result, he was set free by the chief, adopted by the tribe, and given the necessary provisions for his people back in Jamestown. It was the start of a lifelong friendship with Pocahontas, who became a frequent visitor to Jamestown.

She was later baptised as Rebecca and married John Rolfe, Smith's lieutenant, who was born in Heacham (B30), Norfolk. He taught her to speak English and, in 1615, brought her to London with their son, and Pocahontas was received at court by Queen Anne of Denmark, wife of James I. Undoubtedly, their marriage brought about a much easier relationship between the Indians and the early settlers. Sadly, at the age of 21, Pocahontas contracted smallpox and died on board ship in the River Thames. She was buried in St. George's Church, Gravesend (B7). (The story of Pocahontas has been fantasised in two animated films made by the Walt Disney Company.)

In 1727, the town of Gravesend was gutted by fire and St.George's was badly destroyed. Many charred bones in the church were re-interred in a common grave. The church was later converted into the Chapel of Unity and restored by Lady Nancy Astor and reconsecrated in 1952 as a memorial to the Princess. Outside the church is a bronze statue of Pocahontas, presented by the Governor of Virginia, a replica of a statue which stands in Jamestown. Inside the building are two memorial windows and other records relating to her. The son of the Princess and John Rolfe was brought up in Heacham until he left England to return to Virginia.

In 1612, Captain Smith published a map of Virginia. Four years later, he made a voyage during which he first named the area north-east of the Hudson River as New England. In time, he was to become known as the 'father' of the Virginian colony and guided it through its early formative years. The tomb of Captain John

Smith, 'sometime Governor of Virginia and Admirall of New England' (he also fought with some success against the Turks in Transylvania) is in the church of St. Sepulchre, Holborn Viaduct, London. There is also a stained glass window dedicated to his memory in the Services Chapels at Lincoln Cathedral (D10) in the county of his birth.

Lincoln Cathedral is one of the finest medieval buildings in Europe, set high on a hill overlooking the ancient city and dominating the skyline for miles around. St. Hugh's Choir was the first part of the church to be built and St. Hugh, Bishop of Lincoln (1186-122) saw the completion of the choir named after him. The Angel Choir, completed in 1280, houses the shrine of St. Hugh. It is named after the 28 angels carved in stone under the topmost windows. The Wren Library of the Cathedral was designed by Sir Christopher Wren in 1674 for Dean Honywood who had lived in Leiden and had collected many maps, books and documents concerning America. These are still kept in the Library along with a rare collection of manuscripts and early printed books.

Opposite the cathedral is Lincoln Castle where some of the Separatists were tried after they had been captured near Boston. The erection of the castle was ordered by William the Conqueror in 1068. It had a turbulent and chequered history which culminated in the Civil War when on 6 May 1644, the Royalist-held fortress was stormed by Lord Manchester and 650 men were captured. So ended its military history. From the beginning, it had been used as the county jail and in the hall the shire court was held. Of particular interest is the chapel where prisoners were allowed to attend services and the Observatory Tower which affords splendid panoramic views in all directions across the flatlands of Lincolnshire and nearby Nottinghamshire. It also provides an excellent vantage point across the old town to the magnificent west front of the Gothic cathedral.

* * *

As relationships between the English settlers and the Indians began to improve, other eager emigrants began to make the journey across the Atlantic. With the sanction of James I to create settlements in that part of America, two Virginia Companies had been set up, one in Plymouth, mainly made up of people from the West Country, and the other in London. The two companies consisted of groups of merchants who were keen to exploit the opportunities for trade in North America. Finance was made available for the ventures which also gave hope to some of those who had suffered religious persecution.

* * *

During the years when the Pilgrims were in Holland, they were joined by more religious dissidents from England. They heard of the lands which were opening up in Virginia for the establishment of new colonies. They also considered their situation in Holland. As their children grew up, many were tempted by the pleasures offered by life in a city. The 12-year truce between Catholic Spain and the United Provinces, including Holland, was due to run out in 1621. This could well be detrimental to their way of life. Long discussions took place between the Pilgrims as to the suitability, wisdom and cost of undertaking the perilous journey to the New World.

To some, including John Robinson, the appeal of a life across the Atlantic was growing stronger. At first, they considered Guiana but felt it might be too hot and unhealthy as well as already being under Dutch rule. Other settlements governed by Spain might be threatening. But what about Virginia? Perhaps this would offer the best opportunities for the Leiden community? They decided to ask the Virginia Company for sponsorship, and in 1617 John Carver and Robert Cushman, a former member of the Ancient Brethren who had joined the Leiden church, were selected to travel to London to start discussions with the Virginia Company.

Carver was born in Doncaster (D20), South Yorkshire, circa 1575 and was married to John Robinson's sister-in-law, Catherine White. Cushman came from the beautiful city of Canterbury (B5). Canterbury's magnificent cathedral had been regarded as the mother church of Christianity in England since the 12th century. In 1170, the murder of Archbishop Thomas à Becket took place in the cathedral. From then on it was regarded as a shrine of the martyr, attracting many thousands of pilgrims. Robert Cushman had a grocery business at No. 13 The Parade and married Sarah Jekel in St. Alphege's Church – now known as the Canterbury Centre which holds local displays and exhibitions. Sarah had previously lived in the Precincts, just behind No. 59 Palace Street which was regarded by some as an inn. By tradition, it was here that Robert Cushman transacted the hire of the *Mayflower* on behalf of the Pilgrims, though it may well have been in London. In 1603, Robert was excommunicated by the Established Church for refusing to attend recognised Church services. He stood trial before the Church Court in the historic St. Margaret's Church in 1605 (this building now houses a re-creation of Geoffrey Chaucer's *The Canterbury Tales* about earlier pilgrims to the city) before spending time in the cells of the city's Westgate, now an armoury museum. A son, Thomas, was born to the Cushmans in 1607 and in the following year they left Canterbury to join the Ancient Brethren in Amsterdam.

On Carver and Cushman's arrival in London in 1617, they were very favourably welcomed by the Virginia Company and their proposed scheme soon received the sanction of the King. He did, however, suggest that they first contact the Archbishop of Canterbury and the Bishop of London. For obvious reasons, they chose to ignore this. A patent was granted to the Separatists by the Virginia Company in February 1619 and they decided to seek other people, including tradesmen, who might like the opportunity of emigrating.

Unfortunately, a major setback was caused by a book called the *Perth Assembly* which had been produced by the Pilgrim Press in Leiden in early 1619. Any publication which undermined the Church of England was outlawed by King James. This did not deter William Brewster and he continued to print literature opposed to the Church's rigid opposition to Nonconformity. The book was brought to the King's attention. Its basis was a controversial stand against the Established Church on behalf of Scottish Presbyterians by a man named David Calderwood who sent it to

Brewster in Leiden. Copies of the book were shipped back to Scotland and found their way to the Church authorities. A warrant for the arrest of Calderwood and his helpers was issued and by July the printing of the article had been traced back to William Brewster. Brewster went into hiding. Calderwood managed to escape to Holland.

However, King James was determined that the printing press in Leiden should be seized along with any printed matter. A representative party set out to grab the press and take Brewster. He managed to avoid capture but, in his stead, his colleague and sponsor of the printing press, Thomas Brewer, was arrested. It was suggested that he be sent to England for interrogation. Eventually, after much wrangling by the Leiden University authorities, it was agreed that Brewer appear before King James, on condition that he go to England as a free man, he would not be punished, that the King would pay his travelling expenses, and, afterwards, he would be allowed to return to Holland. In the event, the King refused to pay Brewer's costs for the return journey.

The whole incident proved unfortunate as it made the King change his mind about allowing the Leiden Pilgrims to settle in the new colony in America. An alternative plan was put to another body called the New Netherlands Company by John Robinson and they agreed to sponsor the group and provide them with a place to settle on the banks of the Hudson River. A petition was put forward on their behalf to the Prince of Orange on two occasions but was ignored.

In desperation, Robinson started discussions with Thomas Weston, a London-based trader whom he had met in Leiden. Weston promised to help and assured him that he and other merchants might sponsor the undertaking. Meanwhile, William Brewster, still a hunted man, continued to stay out of sight. The Pilgrims could only hope and pray that all would be well.

CHAPTER 6

Return to England

DESPITE THEIR EARLIER DISAPPOINTMENTS, John Carver and Robert Cushman agreed to approach Sir Edwin Sandys, head of the Virginia Company, who was an old friend of the Brewster family. It was through William Brewster's past work as Master of the King's Postes at Scrooby that he first had dealings with Sandys who was the son of the Archbishop of York. He was a man able to use his influence with King James.

Sir Edwin sent them a positive response stating that the Council for Virginia might accept their request. He had successfully put the case of the Leiden Pilgrims to one of the King's Secretaries of State as well as the Archbishop of York. However, the Privy Council referred the request to the Church of England who would not agree to the Pilgrims' requests. The matter dragged on and the King grew tired of the constant approaches he received from the Leiden group in Holland. Eventually, he agreed to allow them to settle in an overseas colony provided they used peaceable methods and did not undermine his authority in any way.

By the year 1620 there were three different English companies with authority to grant lands to any groups who wished to found colonies in America. These were the Plymouth Company, the London Company and the Virginia Company. The first two were chartered by the Crown in 1606, the Plymouth Company being made up of people from the West Country whose intention was to develop the northern part of Virginia. The London Company's aim was to set up a settlement in the south. The companies were popularly known as the Merchant Adventurers and they undertook to finance the Leiden Pilgrims to set up a colony in the northern part of Virginia.

Thomas Weston, whom John Robinson had earlier approached, was at the forefront of negotiations with the Pilgrims.

The Merchant Adventurers had appointed as Treasurer one Christopher Martin, who was to accompany the colonists to the New World. Weston and Martin were to act as negotiators on behalf of the Adventurers. The Pilgrims from the Leiden group were represented by Robert Cushman and John Carver.

Christopher Martin came from Billericay (B17) in Essex. By tradition, he lived at the ancient Chantry House, now a restaurant, in the High Street. The town developed in the 13th century and had a market charter by 1253. The parish church was annexed to the neighbouring church of St. Mary Magdalen in Great Burstead (B17) just over a mile away. Martin was churchwarden there between 1611 and 1612 and it was where he married a widow, Mary Prower, in February 1607. There is a Billerica (F28) in Massachusetts, New England, named after its English counterpart.

Meanwhile, the Merchant Adventurers, through Weston, had commissioned a boat – the 180-ton *Mayflower* – which had docked at Rotherhithe (B10), just over a mile upstream from Greenwich in the Port of London, after a journey from La Rochelle in France on the 23 May 1620. It had already undergone a number of hazardous journeys and proved to be a most seaworthy vessel. Although there is still some uncertainty about its origins, the vessel is generally assumed to have been built at Harwich (B21), Essex. (It is also worthy of note that a ship of the same name was built at Blakeney (B29) in Norfolk, a thriving seaport and shipbuilding centre in the 16th century.) By 1620, the Harwich vessel was already past its prime, having been used mainly for the transportation of wine from France and the Mediterranean to King's Lynn (B31). It is most probable that this *Mayflower* was the same one offered by the town of King's Lynn in service against the Spanish Armada and it is thought to be the same boat which carried the Pilgrims to the New World.

Master of the *Mayflower* was Captain Christopher Jones who had already crossed the Atlantic to transport herds of cattle to Virginia in the 75-ton *Falcon*. He was an experienced and trusted sailor who could be relied upon to take charge of the undertaking to convey the Separatists and other passengers to the New World.

These now fell into two distinct groups. The original Separatists (Pilgrims) – those who were seeking freedom of conscience – and the Adventurers – made up mainly of merchants. Christopher Martin, appointed the ship's Governor, fell into the second category.

Captain Christopher Jones was born circa 1570 in Harwich and his house at number 21 King's Head Street can still be seen close to the harbour. It is a double-fronted two-storey dwelling, beautifully restored, and has an information plaque on the wall. He married Sarah, the seventeen-year-old daughter of Thomas Twitt, a wealthy ship owner and innkeeper in the town. The marriage took place at the church of St. Mary's, Harwich, a few days before Christmas in 1593. That church was demolished in 1819, and three years later the present edifice was erected. A copy of Jones's marriage entry may still be seen by prior arrangement in St. Mary's. Sarah died ten years later and Christopher married a twenty-year-old widow, Josian Gray, daughter of Captain Thomas Thompson of Harwich. Jones played a prominent role in local affairs and became a freeman of the borough in 1601. He followed his father to sea and by 1609 had command of the *Mayflower* in which he owned a quarter share.

The town of Harwich has a long maritime history and is full of interesting back alleys running off the waterfront. It has long been a packet port with the Hook of Holland to which regular ferry services ply. The 17th-century treadmill crane preserved on the quay is probably the only one still in existence and was originally used to service Royal Navy ships. The Port of Harwich Maritime Museum, housed in the old Low Lighthouse on Harwich Green, is dedicated to the Navy, Lifeboat Service and shipping. The old High Lighthouse contains a wireless museum. Just off the Quay, overlooking the spot where the *Mayflower* would have been anchored, is the Ha'penny Pier Visitor Centre. This houses an interesting exhibition – 'Harwich and the New World'.

In about 1610 Captain Christopher Jones moved with his wife and family to London and settled in Rotherhithe on the south bank of the River Thames. It was to be his home for the remainder of his life. His first mate and pilot on the *Mayflower* was John Clarke, and the part-owners of the ship, John Moore and Richard Gardiner, also lived in the area. However, the person who had the largest share in the ship was a Merchant Adventurer named Thomas Goff. After discussions with Captain Jones, Goff offered the *Mayflower* to Thomas Weston for use by the Pilgrims and Adventurers who were aiming to settle in the New World. It was agreed that the *Mayflower* would rendezvous at West Quay, Southampton (A7) with the Leiden Pilgrims who would be shipped from Holland across the English Channel.

Thomas Weston was an ironmonger in the City of London, an astute businessman with a reputation for driving a hard bargain. It was therefore not unusual that in his dealings with the Leiden group, money should be at the forefront of his thinking. He advised the Leiden Pilgrims to beware of the Virginia Company and Dutch authorities, and that he personally would ensure their safe passage to America and their well-being on arrival. Taking him at his word, the Pilgrims drew up an agreement for the mission and Weston duly returned to England with the document.

The agreement signed by the Pilgrims in Leiden included eleven articles. In the main, these dealt with the rating, in monetary terms, of anyone over the age of sixteen, and the financial implications of their stay in Virginia. It was to be an undertaking of at least seven years' duration and included such aspects as employment by way of farming the land, planting of crops, house-building and fishing. It also stipulated that, at the end of the seven years, the land and housing should still be available for the Pilgrims and that food and provisions be made available for them from the general stores. The final article stated that the Pilgrims would be entitled to two days a week to pursue their own employment or interests. This included the Sabbath day which would be entirely taken up with prayers, Bible study and following their own form of religious services.

However, when Weston reached London, two major amendments were made without consultation with the Pilgrims. The first

stipulated that at the end of the seven years, the capital and prof-
its would be equally divided between the Merchant Adventurers
and the Pilgrims. The second amendment was actually the deletion
of the final article which referred to the granting of two days each
week for the Pilgrims to follow their independent activities.
Naturally, John Robinson and the Leiden Pilgrims strongly
protested. Unfortunately, the situation with a number of the
Pilgrims, some of whom had already sold their homes and termi-
nated their employment, was becoming desperate. After hurried
discussions, it was agreed that William Bradford, Edward
Winslow, Isaac Allerton and Samuel Fuller should collectively
write to John Carver and Robert Cushman, their negotiators in
England, insisting that the original articles be re-instated. Despite
this setback, the Pilgrims had great faith and always maintained
that 'God was on their side' and, as they were a wholly united
group, all would be well.

At this stage, news arrived in Holland that other Separatists
from England had heard of the Leiden Pilgrims' plans to emigrate
to the New World and wished to join them. John Robinson readily
agreed to this request.

In response to the letter from the Leiden group, Cushman stated that the Adventurers had reckoned on 150 persons being transported to the New World but, unless the Pilgrims agreed to the
amended articles, they would be short of funding by about £400.
(This was due to the withdrawal from the investment by one of the
Adventurers who objected to the Pilgrims' stipulations.) The good
news was that arrangements were in hand to obtain the *Mayflower*.

The plan was that when the Leiden Pilgrims were shipped to
Southampton they would be joined by more Separatists from
London and other parts of England for their journey to America.
They then had no real alternative but to accept the articles in the
amended agreement, but it was a most unsatisfactory arrangement
from the Pilgrims' point of view.

Weston also sent word from London that news had just been
received that a new grant of land had been given by King James
for a large part of northern Virginia, earlier named New England

by Captain John Smith in 1614, to be separated from the existing colonies in the same part of America. As the Adventurers privately assumed that they might be rewarded by monies made from the lucrative fishing industry around America's eastern seaboard, Weston suggested to the Pilgrims that they consider settling in Virginia. An offer by Captain John Smith to give advice about the Atlantic journey and, indeed, accompany the Pilgrims to help them settle in America was refused. This was perhaps foolish as he was an experienced sailor and soldier and knew the area well. He could have proved useful.

Finally, the Leiden Pilgrims found what they thought would be a suitable ship of their own to take them, first to England, then to North America. Through the sale of their possessions and their properties in Leiden, they were able to raise the finance to purchase the vessel. The *Speedwell* was a boat of 60 tons and berthed at Delfshaven (E4) on the Maese (between Rotterdam and Schiedam), now absorbed into Rotterdam, situated about 24 miles (39 kilometres) from Leiden. Their intention was not only for the *Speedwell* to convey them to North America but also, after arriving there, to be used for fishing purposes.

The time came for the Leiden Pilgrims to make their journey to the port of Delfshaven where the *Speedwell* would be waiting to convey them to England to join with other Separatists and Merchant Adventurers. It must have been an emotional occasion for the would-be emigrants as they bade farewell to those relatives and friends who would not be going with them. Their pastor and leader, John Robinson, had earlier arranged a final get-together at his home, though he himself was not destined to travel with them. He addressed those who were about to leave, imploring them to make friends and work together for the common good with those Pilgrims who

Oude Kerk, Delfshaven

would be joining them at Southampton (A13). According to Edward Winslow's journal '....they that stayed at Leiden feasted us that were to go, at our pastor's house, being large, where we refreshed ourselves, after tears, with singing of psalms, making joyful melody in our hearts, as well with the voice, there being many in our congregation very expert in music'.

Pastor John Robinson stayed in Leiden to continue his ministry with those remaining behind and intended to follow the Pilgrims to the New World at a later date. Sadly, he died in 1625 before he could do so.

The Pilgrims had spent nearly twelve years in Leiden, the last three of which had been taken up with negotiations for arranging their departure for America. When they had first arrived from Amsterdam, they had barely 100 followers but by 1620 this figure had increased fourfold. They must have felt frustrated by the constant problems and set-backs which arose. It was certainly a time for re-assurance but they trusted in God to see them through.

William Bradford had been given charge of the group and, on leaving Leiden, recorded 'So they lefte ye goodly and pleasante citie, which had been their resting place near twelve years; but they were pilgrimes....' The last phrase refers to the Christian's life on earth as a pilgrimage to heaven. It is from this particular quote that the name 'Pilgrim Fathers' is thought to have originated.

On Friday 21 July, the Pilgrims who were to make the journey, supported by many friends and well-wishers from both Leiden and Amsterdam, went along the Kloksteeg to the Rapenburg Quay to board boats that would carry them along the waterways to Delfshaven (E4). The journey was via the Vliet river, passing The Hague and Delft (E3) (a town famous for its pottery and the burial place of Dutch monarchs), then on by the Schie river to Delfshaven. The *Speedwell* was waiting at the harbourside in readiness for the journey across the English Channel.

At the time of the Pilgrims, Delfshaven was a port used by the East India Company. Legend has it that, prior to their departure, the Pilgrims worshipped in the Oude Kerk. Situated on the quayside and built in 1417 as St. Anthonius Chapel, it was converted in the 16th century into a cruciform church in late-Gothic style. The front was heightened in 1761, renewed in Regency style and a wooden clock tower built behind it. A carillon of bells peals out every quarter of an hour. Inside the church is a Bätz-Witte organ and next to the choir is an outbuilding which houses the vestry and the Pilgrim Fathers memorial. In 1992 the church was handed over to the Foundation for Old Dutch Churches and a restoration plan was launched. It is situated at No. 20 Aelbrechtskolk and Dutch Reformed Church services are held every Sunday.

On the front of the Oude Kerk are two plaques – one which gives the history of the church and the other states it was the departure point of the *Speedwell* on which the Pilgrim Fathers sailed to England on 1 August 1620. If you stroll along the quay passing former merchants' houses, town dwellings and a colourful flotilla of boats on the canal, it is not difficult to imagine the scene as John Robinson bade a last farewell to his Pilgrim friends.

Delfshaven is now a colourful suburb of the city of Rotterdam but was once a separate community. It is the only part of the central area of the city to have survived the bombing of the Second World War. In 1389 the City of Delft was granted permission to dig a canal from the River Schie to the Meuse to establish its own seaport, Delfshaven. In the 15th century it grew into a community with its own trade and industry and only became a part of Rotterdam in 1886. In 1577, Piet Hein, a naval hero, was born in Delfshaven. In 1628, near Cuba, he conquered a Spanish fleet with silver treasure on board.

Once the Leiden Pilgrims had boarded the *Speedwell*, they must have felt a mixture of anticipation and sadness as they waited for a suitable tide to start their journey. When the master of the *Speedwell*, Captain Reynolds, signalled that the time had finally come to depart, John Robinson and his companions on the harbourside knelt down in prayer for a safe journey for the ship and its passengers. Slowly it moved out of Delfshaven harbour into the stream and headed for the open sea. Their momentous journey had begun. Yet there were many problems to overcome before they would finally reach their planned destination.

CHAPTER 7

Final Departure

TERMS OF THE CHARTER for the *Mayflower* stated that the transaction would be for a journey from London, via Southampton, across the Atlantic to the area around the mouth of the Hudson River, then returning to Rotherhithe.

Rotherhithe is in the London borough of Southwark (B10), a place which has played a vital role in Britain's maritime history. The area is dominated by the tower of Southwark Cathedral which had its origins in Anglo Saxon times. It was then known as St. Mary Overie. In 1212 there was a disastrous fire which badly damaged the church and only a few traces of Norman work have survived. The new church was built in the Gothic style with pointed arches, much of the work taking place between 1220-73. After another fire in the late 14th century the tower and rebuilding of the south transept were finally completed by 1420. Under Henry VIII, the building also became the parish church of St. Saviour, Southwark. It was finally elevated to the rank of cathedral in the mid-19th century.

The church has important American links in that John Harvard was born in Southwark in 1607, and baptised in St. Saviour's (see chapter 12). He is commemorated by the Harvard Chapel, just off the north transept. Southwark Cathedral contains a number of other important tombs and memorials including one to William Shakespeare whose brother, Edmund, was buried there in 1607. The cathedral is quite close to the Globe Theatre which has been brilliantly reconstructed. It was the brainchild of American actor and director Sam Wanamaker (1913-93) who had a dream of re-building the Globe as near as possible to its original site and design. He is commemorated by a wall plaque in Southwark Cathedral.

After a visit to the cathedral the visitor should walk along

Clink Street, off Bankside. Here stood the Clink Prison which gave rise to the term 'in clink' for describing someone in jail. The name was given to a number of prisons that stood in that vicinity. In 1824, the father of Charles Dickens was imprisoned for debt for three months at the nearby Marshalsea jail. This stood on the site of the present John Harvard Library at 211 Borough High Street. Much of Dickens' novel *Little Dorrit* is set within the borough of Southwark. As a young boy Charles had lodgings in Lant Street and later used his landlord and landlady as models for Mr. and Mrs. Garland in *The Old Curiosity Shop*. The first prison in Southwark in 1127 was a cellar in the Palace of the Bishop of Winchester, (remains of this, with its fine 14th-century rose window, can still be seen in Clink Street, by St. Mary Overie Dock where the full-scale prototype of the *Golden Hind*, mentioned earlier in chapter 2, is moored. This vessel, like the original, has circumnavigated the globe). The last prison was in Deadman's Place (now Park Street). The prison held Protestant and Catholic religious martyrs at various times until it was burned down in 1780 by anti-Catholic rioters. Clink Prison Museum in Clink Street has a fascinating exhibition of London's unsavoury past.

If visitors are looking for something a little more sinister or horrific they should visit the London Dungeon in nearby Tooley Street. Here can be seen items of torture and vivid re-creations of some of the most gory incidents in England's history.

What was once the Pilgrim Fathers' Memorial Church is situated on Great Dover Street at the junction with Spurgeon Street. It is a modern rather unpretentious place with no sense of history, built in 1956, backing onto a council estate. It has been taken over by a community group and turned into flats. However, the archives are available for research purposes.

Mayflower Memorial, Southampton

Rotherhithe is situated about three kilometres down the Thames from Southwark and the departure point of the *Mayflower* can still be seen close by the present Mayflower Inn. It is understood that the name Rotherhithe is derived from two Saxon words, 'rethra', a sailor, and 'hythe', a landing place. Today it is part of the Docklands Development Scheme and many changes have taken place over recent years.

The parish church of St. Mary the Virgin is the second on the site, the original dating from 1282. The building is situated on a narrow street near to the river surrounded by stark warehouses, some of which have been converted for modern uses, opposite a former charity school founded in 1703 by Peter Hills, a 'Brother' of Trinity House which ran the coastguard and pilot services. It was at St. Mary the Virgin church that Captain Jones who captained the *Mayflower* and some of the Pilgrims worshipped before leaving for Southampton. The original church was demolished in 1714 to make way for the present brick-built building. Lists of bills, craftsmen and subscribers are preserved in the Southwark Local Studies Library. The tower was added in 1747. Captain Christopher Jones had two of his children baptised in St. Mary's. John Clarke and Richard Gardiner were also married there. Jones was buried in the churchyard of the original church after his death on 5 March 1622 but his last resting place can no longer be identified. There is a memorial tablet to Captain Jones on the eastern wall inside the church and a modern statue of him in the churchyard.

Almost opposite the church is the Mayflower Inn on Rotherhithe Street. In the 17th century the inn was known as The Shippe and was patronised by mariners as well as locals. It is likely that some of the crew and merchants who sailed on the *Mayflower* would have used the place. Until a few years ago, it was also licensed as a post office and was the only pub in Great Britain to sell British and American stamps. It has some lovely oak panelling and is full of maritime memorabilia including information relating to the Pilgrim Fathers. In the first floor restaurant, the visitor can see a copy of the passenger list for the *Mayflower*. It is also possible to stand on the balcony outside the pub and gaze down river to the historic quayside.

Whilst in the area, the visitor should make his way along Rotherhithe Street to the riverside at Cumberland Wharf where there is a modern tribute to the Pilgrim Fathers represented in two statues by Peter MacLean. They are called Sunbeam Weekly and The Pilgrim's Pocket and depict a Pilgrim Father looking into a young boy's comic paper. If you take a peek over the boy's shoulder you will see that the publication contains a montage of modern American inventions and sites plus a depiction of the *Mayflower*.

One can imagine the bustle and excitement in 1620 as the *Mayflower* finally left Rotherhithe. Its passengers – Adventurers and Pilgrims – would have varying reasons for setting off on a journey which, for many, would end in the New World. Others were to return home disillusioned before they even made the Atlantic crossing.

By tradition, the *Mayflower* sailed down river passing Greenwich and then headed north across the Thames Estuary to pick up a contingent of passengers from Essex. These included the group which first assembled at the Chantry House in Billericay, home of Christopher Martin, before proceeding overland to Leigh-on-Sea (B18) to join the *Mayflower*. Leigh-on-Sea is an old fishing village on the Essex coastline with a cobbled High Street and fishermen's cottages, weatherboarded against the elements. It is situated in an elevated position looking across the wide estuary of the Thames. The *Mayflower* then sailed round the coast of Kent and followed the south coast to Southampton.

* * *

After a three-day voyage from Delfshaven, the *Speedwell*, bringing the Leiden Pilgrims, entered The Solent, passing the Isle of Wight (A14). It arrived in Southampton on 26 July and berthed alongside the *Mayflower* which was already tied up at West Quay.

Southampton (A13) in the early 17th century was a small walled town with just a few dwellings outside its perimeter. To enter the town, one had to pass through one of the main gateways such as the fortified Bargate or Eastgate. The latter is situated where the rivers Test and Itchen converge to meet Southampton Water. This is a natural harbour which led to its development as the major English port for trans-Atlantic sea crossings.

* * *

Despite extensive damage caused during the Second World War, there is still much to see from Southampton's past. The old town has a number of links with the Pilgrims which are worth exploring. Perhaps the parish church of St. Michael's is a good starting point as the surrounding square, once used for markets, has much atmosphere and formed the centre of the town's French Quarter. The church was founded about 1070, and parts of the tower date from that period. Its spire served as a landmark for sailors from the 15th century. Opposite is the Tudor House, the finest half-timbered structure in Southampton and once a rich merchant's town house, which now serves as a museum. To the rear is a garden laid out in a medieval style. Beyond is an almost intact Norman merchant's house, believed to have been built around 1150.

Westgate would have been familiar to the Pilgrims as they would have passed through it on their way from West Quay into the town. The gate once opened directly onto the waterfront of the River Test and it was from here that King Henry v sailed for Agincourt in 1415. On the south side of Westgate is the half-timbered Tudor Merchants' Hall which originally stood in St. Michael's Square and was used as a Woollen Cloth Hall. It was sold in 1634 and re-erected in its present position for use as a warehouse. An original warehouse which survives from the medieval period is the Wool House, originally erected by monks from nearby Beaulieu Abbey, now a superb maritime museum. It houses a specially poignant exhibition telling the story of the *Titanic*. Four days after leaving Ocean Dock on 12 April 1912 on its maiden voyage, the liner was struck by an iceberg causing it to sink within a matter of two and a half hours. 1,500 of the 2,224 people on board lost their lives.

Our particular interest must take us within the shadow of the old walls outside the Westgate into Western Esplanade to see the Mayflower Memorial, a tall stone column standing near the spot where the Pilgrim Fathers embarked for America. The memorial was erected in 1913 to commemorate the sailing of the *Mayflower* and the *Speedwell* from the West Quay in 1620. It has plaques attached by the Mayflower Descendants Society.

The Pilgrim Fathers are also commemorated by the Mayflower Park which occupies the site of the old West Quay where the *Mayflower* was moored. It looks out over the Test estuary between Town Quay and Western Docks and is the site of the annual Southampton Boat Show. It is one of the best viewing points for ships which use the docks. Mayflower Park is also close to the modern Ocean Village development with its marina, speciality shops and restaurants alongside the waterfront. Southampton is known as the home of the Cunard liners which plied back and forth across the Atlantic, especially great ships such as the *Mauretania*, *Queen Mary*, *Queen Elizabeth* and the *QEii*.

* * *

The *Speedwell* was about a third of the size of the *Mayflower*. A week had already been lost by the *Mayflower* whilst it waited for the *Speedwell* to arrive from Holland. When it moored, there was an enthusiastic meeting between the Pilgrims from Leiden and those who had travelled from Rotherhithe and Essex. As well as discussing mutual hopes and fears there was an overriding bond between the groups. Both had great faith in God and a true sense of mission.

Notwithstanding, there were still some matters to be settled before the two ships could set sail. For a start, there was the unsolved question as to what the terms were to be regarding their settlement in the New World. The Leiden Pilgrims were unhappy with those already agreed in London by Thomas Weston on their behalf. On that occasion, they had been represented at the negotiations by John Carver and Robert Cushman. When questioned, both had appeared vague and Carver stated that he was in Southampton when the terms were being drawn up in London. Cushman argued that he had agreed to obtain finance in London and, afterwards, forward it to Southampton to cover the cost of the ships' provisions. It had not arrived and this meant there was a shortfall in the amount of money required to cover the cost of the journey.

Weston arrived in Southampton to witness the departure of the two ships. When cornered by the Pilgrims, he stubbornly refused to change the original agreement with them. Rightly, they emphasised that the agreement had been that no amendments would be made without the full approval of the Leiden group. Clearly, the terms of the agreement had not been followed. On being challenged, Weston told them they must 'stand on their own legs', and departed in a temper, leaving them to their own resources.

The Pilgrims now had to raise more capital to pay for provisions. This was finally achieved by the sale of a surplus stock of butter. They wrote to the Merchant Adventurers to confirm final arrangements and explain their shortfall in supplies. These would be essential not only for the voyage but also when they arrived in the New World. An offer was made that if the project was successful in the seven years of the contract, the Pilgrims would agree to an extension of the profit-sharing arrangement, provided the Adventurers agreed to all other points in the original agreement. The final part of the letter explained the additional cost they had run up, caused mainly through the delay in waiting whilst the matter was settled.

An encouraging letter then arrived from John Robinson, the pastor in Leiden, and was read out to the Pilgrims. It really was a form of sermon which gave them much food for thought for their long journey and for the future. He stated that 'they should all consider their sins and shortcomings every day and they must try and understand that God sometimes puts his faithful followers through hard and dangerous missions. They were to seek His guidance; be of good behaviour; be charitable to strangers whom they might meet; work for the common good of all; and elect a Civil Government from among themselves'. It was to be John Robinson's last letter to them.

The Pilgrims agreed that during the journey they should elect a governor and two or three assistants for each ship who would have overall authority. Christopher Martin, the undisputed leader of the London group, was elected Governor of the *Mayflower* with Robert Cushman as an Assistant. John Carver was appointed as Governor of the *Speedwell*.

Despite earlier problems with the *Speedwell*, both ships were ready to sail on 5 August 1620, and the Pilgrims were on their way at last. However, it was not long before the *Speedwell* sprang a leak and Captain Reynolds declared he dare not proceed into the open sea. The problem was serious. There was no chance of them braving the Atlantic with the ship in such a poor state. Carver signalled to the *Mayflower* which quickly came alongside. Captain Jones suggested they put in to the nearest harbour for examination of the damage and to see to repairs. The most appropriate place was Dartmouth (A6) in Devon. They entered the harbour at Bayard's Cove exactly a week after leaving Southampton.

* * *

Situated at the western side of the beautiful estuary of the River Dart, Dartmouth is one of the most picturesque and interesting old towns in England. Its deep sheltered harbour provides safe anchorage. Today, the river is fringed with rocky coves of red sandstone, churches, castles and gardens. Buildings rise steeply from the Waterfront and overlooking the whole town in a commanding position is the Britannia Royal Naval College. The building was completed in 1905 to the plans of Sir Aston Webb, and is where officer cadets are trained for active service. In the past, these have included members of the Royal family such as George V, Edward VIII, George VI and both Prince Charles and Prince Andrew. It was also the place where Queen Elizabeth II was first introduced to Prince Philip when he was an officer cadet.

The Royal Avenue Gardens is a good starting place to explore the narrow streets of Dartmouth with its wealth of merchants houses from the 16th and 17th centuries. Parts of the Quay were built on land reclaimed from the sea between 1588 and 1640 to meet the requirements of the Newfoundland fishing trade. Just off the Quay is Victoria Road and on the right is the famous Butterwalk, originally built between 1635 and 1640 and restored after Second World War bombing. This group of buildings includes Dartmouth Museum which has an interesting display of maritime history, including the Pilgrim Fathers.

The *Mayflower* and the *Speedwell* anchored in Bayard's Cove whilst repairs took place to the latter. There are two plaques on the quay to commemorate where the Speedwell was moored and other links with the Pilgrims. The surrounding area has attractive old houses with the Customs House of 1739 fronting the cobbled pavement. It is often used for filming and was the location of some of the scenes in the memorable British television series *The Onedin Line*. Just a few yards along the adjoining Lower Street is the Harbour Bookshop. This was established in 1951 by Christopher Milne, the original Christopher Robin in the book *When We Were Very Young* and the various *Winnie the Pooh* publications. He was the son of children's writer, A.A. Milne.

Following South Town to the river mouth we can see splendid views across the charming inlet of Warfleet Creek. Beyond, are walks through the Castle Estate to Dartmouth Castle and the Church of St. Petrox. The castle was first fortified by John Hawley in 1388 and from it stones and bolts were hurled at enemy ships. The nearby church has origins in the 6th century and stands sentinel at the entrance to the estuary with densely wooded hills on either side.

On the opposite side of the Dart estuary is the twin stronghold of the privately-owned Kingswear Castle (A6). Once, a great chain, supported by six boats, was slung across the river between the two castles as a defence against hostile vessels. These days, visitors can enjoy boat trips up or down this lovely river starting at the South Embankment quay and sailing as far as the ancient market town and river port of Totnes (A5). In summer months, Totnes holds a colourful Elizabethan-style weekly market, peopled by costumed characters, and this is held on the forecourt of the Civic Hall every Tuesday.

* * *

It must have been frustrating for the Pilgrims as they waited until repairs to the hull of the *Speedwell* had been made. Although the weather was good, further delay could bring the possibility of strong winds and storms as winter approached.

Eventually, on 23 August, taking advantage of the fine weather, both ships left Dartmouth and headed down the English Channel passing Land's End. But after they had travelled 300 miles (450 kilometres), Captain Reynolds of the *Speedwell* again found his ship was in trouble and hove in alongside the *Mayflower*. Not only did the two captains, their mates and craftsmen have a set-to about the situation but some of the principal passengers joined in as well. There was no alternative but to put back into the nearest port to sort out the situation once and for all. Captain Jones led them back to the Devon seaport of Plymouth, heading round Drake's Island and Plymouth Hoe to Sutton Pool harbour.

After examination, it was declared that if the *Speedwell* was to be made thoroughly seaworthy, it would be necessary to re-rig the ship, a task which would take some days. Apart from the time factor, there was also the cost of delay which would have to be borne by the Pilgrims. This they could not afford. Eventually, it was agreed there was no alternative but for the *Speedwell* to be left behind to be sold. At least any monies made from the sale might be used by the Pilgrims to help pay outstanding debts for earlier repair work. Yet there was no way in which the *Mayflower* could take on board all of the passengers of the other ship. The problem was partly overcome when eighteen passengers on the Speedwell decided to abandon the journey and stay behind. Among these was Robert Cushman and his family who had become sick of the whole business. Once the ship had been repaired, it would return to London with those passengers who wished to return.

During the time the Pilgrims and Adventurers were in Plymouth, many townsfolk came along to offer friendship and hospitality. Some were Nonconformists like themselves and in sympathy with their cause.

Meanwhile, there was much to do to prepare for the Atlantic journey in the *Mayflower*. Extra provisions needed to be loaded aboard, accommodation to be adapted to cope with the extra number of passengers, and a general check over the ship's seaworthiness was also necessary. As the days went by, all were concerned for their safety if they left it too late to leave before the onset of bad weather. It was a soul-searching time for everyone. As far as the Pilgrims were concerned, they had set out from Holland and London on a mission and God would see them through to their final destination. The people of Plymouth admired their great faith and optimism.

* * *

Plymouth's location at the head of Plymouth Sound, straggling the estuaries of the Rivers Tamar and Plym, make it a natural choice for a port. By the time the *Mayflower* arrived in Sutton Pool harbour, the city already had a distinguished reputation in seafaring through its past associations with sea captains such as John Hawkins, Francis Drake, Humphrey Gilbert, Martin Frobisher and Walter Raleigh. It was later a regular calling place of Captain James Cook in between his various journeys across the world to Africa, the Pacific, Far East, Australasia and Antarctica. There is still much to see that recalls those glorious years of exploration and success.

In prime position is Plymouth Hoe which has one of the best and most scenic promenades in Europe, overlooking The Sound. It is a marvellous vantage point from which to view maritime craft and boats from the nearby naval base of Devonport on the River Tamar. It was on the Hoe that, according to tradition, Drake completed his game of bowls in 1588 despite the approaching Spanish Armada. His fine statue can be seen in a prime position on the Hoe, looking out to sea. Close by is the Naval War Memorial, a lofty obelisk. Also on the slopes of the Hoe is Smeaton's Tower (lighthouse) which once stood on the Eddystone rock for 120 years before being replaced. Visitors can climb the 93 steps to the top to enjoy breathtaking views across the city and along the coastline. Reminders of Plymouth's military days can also be seen at the Citadel, a proud fortification built during the reign of Charles II.

A modern development is the Plymouth Dome, just below

Smeaton's Tower, a popular heritage centre with inter-active displays which take the visitor through 400 years of the city's history, recalling its many achievements, famous people such as Drake, Cook and the Pilgrim Fathers, and the part played by Plymouth in the nation's history. It is a good starting point to learn more about the city before exploring its many buildings and attractions, both ancient and modern.

The place which attracts attention for sheer historic atmosphere is The Barbican, the section of Sutton Pool harbour which is surrounded by old taverns, warehouses and winding alleys, and with its famous waterfront from which the Pilgrim Fathers finally left England in 1620. The area has dozens of speciality shops, galleries and craft workshops tucked away between the old port buildings. It also has its fair share of charming teashops, eating houses and pubs to prolong a visit. Island House, now occupied by the Tourist Information Centre, is reputed to be where some of the Pilgrims were accommodated during their wait in Plymouth. On the side of the house is a full list of all those who made the journey across the Atlantic which started at the West Quay.

On the quay itself is the Mayflower Memorial and Steps. There is a simple granite stone in the pavement engraved MAYFLOWER 1620 which marks the actual spot where the Pilgrim Fathers embarked. There is also a late-Victorian memorial tablet placed in the sea-wall at West Pier in 1891. Since 1934, it has been protected by a classical portico and displays the Union Jack and the Stars and Stripes simultaneously. Other plaques relate to some of Plymouth's other historical associations.

The best time to go along to this historic spot is early morning when perhaps a sea mist hovers around the shoreline. If the tide is in, listen to the waves lapping against the harbour wall. Alternatively, make your way to the Hoe in the evening. Gaze out to sea in a south-westerly direction across Plymouth Sound as the sun is going down. Pause for a while in the silence, perhaps only interrupted by the overhead screech of seagulls. It was in that direction that the Pilgrim Fathers finally headed on their 2,800 mile (4,480 kilometres) journey.

Quite close to the Mayflower Memorial is the Elizabethan House, a typical Tudor sea captain's timber-framed house. Other nearby historic places worth a visit are the Prysten House, a late 15th-century building in the city centre, along with St. Andrew's Parish Church, rebuilt in 1957 after the Second World War when much of the city centre was wiped out by devastating air raids.

* * *

The townsfolk of Plymouth had shown much support for the Pilgrims. Indeed, Puritan preachers occupied many pulpits – especially that of St. Andrew's Parish Church – from the year 1600. A number of local people had revolted when they heard that clergymen were being deprived of their livings because of refusing to conform with the Book of Common Prayer. Printed matter condemning the behaviour of the people was brought into the area by local Members of Parliament. In response, the locals had rallied to support the Pilgrims in any way they could, such as offering accommodation, food and other provisions and generally making them feel welcome whilst they were in port. The ship's passengers were also permitted to worship in St. Andrew's Church (badly damaged in the Second World War but beautifully restored and including modern stained glass windows designed by the distinguished post-War artist John Piper).

The Pilgrim Fathers never forgot the kindness and hospitality they received from the people of Plymouth. In the United States of America there are no fewer than 26 towns or cities which bear the name Plymouth.

At long last, on 6 September 1620, the passengers were ferried out to the *Mayflower*. She raised anchor with the crew and 102 passengers including 34 children on board – and sailed into the history books.

CHAPTER 8

Crossing the Atlantic

AS THE MAYFLOWER headed out of Plymouth Sound on 6 September 1620, it steered a south-westerly course to pass Land's End and the Scilly Isles and headed out into the Atlantic. At the outset, the weather was quite good until crosswinds arose and then, according to William Bradford's reminiscences, there came 'many fierce storms with which the ship was shrewdly shaken'. A young man named John Howland was washed overboard in a storm. By extreme good fortune he managed to grab hold of a rope and was able to cling to it until help came. He lived to the ripe old age of eighty.

There was a lot of seasickness amongst both the passengers and crew and the tossing ship would have allowed very little comfort. With the desperate conditions and cold would also have come the fear of illness which was soon to take its toll on the frightened brethren both during and after their journey. Food and provisions deteriorated, while the longer the journey lasted, the more the chance of food poisoning, dysentery and other illnesses became likely. The passengers had to survive by eating hard, mouldy biscuits, rancid butter and drinking brackish water. Everyone was crammed together giving no room whatsoever for personal

The *Mayflower*

privacy. The stench would have been most disagreeable. There were also some goats and other domestic animals on board.

A terrifying ordeal for everyone occurred when the main beam in the middle of the ship bent and cracked. By good fortune or providence, the Pilgrims had on board a 'great screw' – probably a house jack or winch – which they used to hold the mast firmly in place for the rest of the voyage. (It has been speculated that this screw could have been part of a printing press.)

Elizabeth, wife of Stephen Hopkins, gave birth to a son on board ship who was baptised Oceanus. The Hopkins already had four children. There was also a death during the voyage. A young manservant named William Button of Austerfield died towards the end of the journey and was buried at sea – just two days before they finally made landfall.

It is perhaps opportune to take a look at the passengers and crew. This is possible through the writings of William Bradford who left for posterity a vivid account of the voyage and all who sailed in the ship. In his *History of Plimoth Plantation* written between 1630 and 1654, Bradford includes a passenger list. There were a number of family groups amongst the Pilgrims and Adventurers, and others who, for varying reasons, made the journey.

Perhaps one of the most unusual and saddest stories of all relates to a family of four children with the surname More who came from the sleepy little hamlet of Shipton (c7) set deep in the Shropshire countryside. They were born to Samuel and Katherine More of Larden Hall, now demolished, near Shipton, situated between Much Wenlock and the historic town of Ludlow. The couple were cousins and their family had been landowners since the 13th century. Their marriage had been more of a business transaction than a love match in order to unite the two family estates of Larden and Linley, located near to Bishop's Castle (c6) within the same county.

After their fourth child was born, Samuel found out he was not the natural father of any of the children and accused his wife of adultery with a local farm labourer from Brockton in the near-by parish of Stanton Long. Katherine did not deny the charge and, consequently, Samuel took steps to ensure that none of the children would inherit either of the estates and also sued for divorce. The settlement provided that the four minors would be under the control of Samuel and he was then in the position of being able to dispose of the children as he wished.

It was a practice for orphans and abandoned children from London to be transported to the New World to help with the supply of labour in new British colonies. After consultation with a member of the Virginia Company, arrangements were made for the More children to sail from Rotherhithe on the *Mayflower* and the leaders of the Pilgrims agreed to take them under their wing. Elinor More was put in the charge of Edward Winslow and Jasper More of John Carver. Richard and Mary were placed in the care of William Brewster.

A plaque in the little church at Shipton, presented by the Massachusetts Society of Mayflower Descendants, states that each child had been baptised there. The ancient half-timbered building stands next to the Elizabethan Shipton Hall and overlooks the picturesque Corvedale valley, set just below Wenlock Edge, famed in composer Vaughan Williams' suite *On Wenlock Edge*. The plaque states that Jasper and Mary died in 1620, quite probably on the *Mayflower*, whilst Elinor died the following year in Plimoth Plantation. Richard More survived and married Christine Hunter in 1636 and moved to Salem (F27), Massachusetts, where he became a seaman. They had seven children who were all baptised in the settlement. Christine died in 1677, after which Richard remarried, lived to the age of 80 and died in 1695.

Of the other passengers and crew members who sailed on the voyage, there were, firstly, the captain and crew who would be returning to England with the ship – Captain Christopher Jones and four senior mates – John Clarke (pilot); Robert Coppin (pilot); Andrew Williamson; and John Parker. There were also four quartermasters and a surgeon – Dr. Giles Heale – as well as a carpenter, cooks, a cooper, boatswains, gunners and about three dozen deck hands. Four of these had been hired as mariners. John Allerton (aged 21 plus) was hired in London, and thought to have had sympathies with the Separatist movement. Although he was commissioned to return to England to collect the next group of Pilgrims, like so many others he died soon after the arrival of the *Mayflower* in the New World.

The death toll after leaving England and during the first few months in the New World virtually reduced the number of passengers and crew by half. This was caused by a number of things including bad sanitation, rotting food, infection and dysentery on board the *Mayflower*. Many passengers had scurvy due to a deficiency of vitamin C in their food. Others suffered respiratory problems which would have been caused by the extremely damp and cold weather conditions. The many deaths were described as an 'epidemic' and few individuals or family units were not affected in some way. In total, only 54 passengers survived the first year, 21 of them under the age of sixteen.

Also amongst the crew were Thomas English (30), a sailor who died; William Trevor, mariner, whose contract was to stay for twelve months in the new colony, along with another sailor named Ely. Both returned to England at the end of the agreed period. John Alden (21), the cooper, came from Harwich. He stayed on in the New World and married Priscilla Mullins with whom he had eleven children. Their romance was the subject of a poem 'The Courtship of Miles Standish'. Miles Standish also had designs on the fair lady but lost out to John. Eventually, Alden became a leader of the Plymouth colony and died at Duxbury (F21), Massachusetts, in 1687.

Of the passengers on the *Mayflower*, there were ten single men who were perhaps seeking a new life in a new country or possibly had strong religious beliefs as members of the Pilgrim community. Of these, only three survived the epidemic and bad weather conditions.

(N.B. From hereon in this chapter, those people who travelled from Leiden in the *Speedwell* are shown in bold type and those who died within the first year of landing are marked with an asterisk.)

There was Richard Gardiner (20) from Harwich, who eventually died at sea circa 1650; Gilbert Winslow (20), brother of Edward Winslow from Droitwich; and **Peter Browne** (20) who originated from Great Burstead in Essex but who had earlier travelled to Holland to join the Leiden community. He was to marry twice, have four children, and died at Plymouth, New England in 1633.

All the remaining single men had been part of the community in Holland and had been looking forward to establishing the new colony in America. These included – **Richard Britteridge** * (21), from Great Burstead in Essex. He died aboard the *Mayflower* on 21 December 1620 as it lay in Plymouth (F19) harbour in New England, the journey having proved too much for him. There were also **Richard Clarke; Moses Fletcher** (38), a smith from Sandwich (B4) in Kent; **John Goodman** (25), a linen weaver; **Edward Margerson; Digory Priest** * (40), a hatter from London whose wife and children arrived later in New England after his death; and **Thomas Williams** from Yarmouth (B27), Norfolk.

There were a number of family units on board the *Mayflower* which can be divided into 24 households.

1. **Isaac Allerton** (34) was a tailor by profession from London. His first wife was called **Mary** * (32) and their children, **Bartholomew** (8), **Remember** (6) and **Mary** (4). After the death of his first wife in 1621, Isaac married William Brewster's daughter, Fear, who was to arrive at the colony at a later date. They had one son before she died and Isaac married for a third time. He died at New Haven (F1), Connecticut in 1659. The Allerton family were accompanied on the *Mayflower* by **John Hooke** * (14), a servant boy, who died in 1621.

2. John Billington (36) from London, his wife, Ellen (32) and children, Francis (14) and John (8). John Billington proved to be the 'black sheep' of the community. He was a troublemaker, usually at loggerheads with the Pilgrims in many situations for which he was later punished. He was eventually found guilty of murder and hanged in September 1630.

3. Elder **William Bradford** (31) and his wife, **Dorothy May** *

(23). After the death of Governor John Carver in 1621, William Bradford was elected to the office which, apart from a five year gap, he was to hold up to the time of his death at Plymouth, New England on 9 May 1657 at the age of 68. He married for a second time after the death of Dorothy May who drowned in Cape Cod Harbour on 7 December 1620.

4. Elder **William Brewster** (54), his wife, **Mary** (52) and children, **Love** (9) and **Wrestling** (6). With them were two children from the More family – Richard (7) and Mary (4). William Brewster became the Ruling Elder in the community and he died at the age of 77 on 18 April 1643 at Duxbury, New England, one of the new communities established by the Pilgrims. He was to live to see his life's ambition of living in a place of religious freedom come true.

5. Deacon **John Carver** * (54) and his wife **Catherine** (40). John provided initial leadership for the Pilgrims but died at Plymouth, New England, in April 1621 and was succeeded by William Bradford. Accompanying them was **Desire Minter** (20), a ward of Carver's, destined to return to England, and Jasper More (6), another of the More children. With this family group were also three servants – **John Howland** (28) from London who was to marry Elizabeth Tilley, daughter of John Tilley, with whom he had ten children and he died in 1673 at Plymouth, New England; William Latham, a young servant boy who was to spend twenty years in the colony before finally dying of starvation in the Bahamas; and **Roger Wilder** *.

6. **James Chilton** * (57), a tailor who lived near to St. Augustine's Abbey in Canterbury, his wife, **Susannah** * and daughter Mary (15). James died on the *Mayflower* whilst it was still harboured at Cape Cod and his wife was to die a few months later at Plimoth Plantation during the epidemic. Their daughter, Mary, was cared for by other Pilgrims and she eventually married John Winslow, brother of Governor Edward Winslow, and they produced nine children. Mary died at Boston, New England, in 1679.

7. **Francis Cooke** (43), a wool comber, and his son **John** (8).

They were to be joined by the remaining members of the family – his wife and other two children – at a later date. Francis died at Plymouth, New England in 1663. John married and had four children. He died in Dartmouth (F5), New England in 1694. Sir Winston Churchill and US Presidents, Ulysses S. Grant and George Bush, claimed decendency from Francis Cooke.

8. **John Crackston** * (35), originally from Colchester (B20), and his son **John** made up a family unit of two. John Snr. died in the epidemic whilst his son died of exposure seven years later in 1628 at Plymouth, New England, after he got lost in woods in extremely cold weather.

9. **Francis Eaton** (25), carpenter, formerly of Bristol, and his wife **Sarah** * (30). They had an infant, **Samuel**. After Sarah's death, Francis married twice and died at Plymouth in 1633. Samuel eventually married and died at Middleborough (F9), New England in 1648.

10. **Edward Fuller** * (25), formerly of Redenhall (B25) Norfolk, his wife **Anne** * and son **Samuel** (5). Edward and Anne both died in 1621. After the death of his parents, Samuel was cared for by the Pilgrim community and later married. He died in 1683 at Barnstaple, New England (F11).

11. **Dr. Samuel Fuller** (35) was a Deacon and surgeon, born at Redenhall, Norfolk, in 1585. In Leiden he worked as a weaver. His wife followed him across the Atlantic in 1623. Dr. Fuller was accompanied by his manservant, **William Button** * (22) from Austerfield, Yorkshire, who died aboard the *Mayflower* a day or two before its arrival at Cape Cod on 6 November 1620.

12. Stephen Hopkins (35), his wife Elizabeth (20+) and children, Constana (15), Giles (13), Damaris (3) and Oceanus *. Stephen originated from Wotton-under-Edge (A19) in Gloucestershire and joined the Pilgrims in London. He married his second wife, Elizabeth, at St. Mary's Church in London's Whitechapel on 19 February 1617. Stephen died at Plymouth, New England in 1644, Elizabeth circa 1640, and

Giles at Yarmouth (F12), Massachusetts in 1690. Constana died in 1677 at Eastham (F14), New England having borne twelve children, whilst Damaris died at Plymouth, New England circa 1666. Oceanus lived for barely a year. With the Hopkins family were two manservants – Edward Doty (27) and Edward Lester. In his second marriage, Doty produced seven children. He died at Yarmouth, New England in 1655. Lester eventually moved to Virginia and died there.

13. Christopher Martin *(45) Treasurer to the Pilgrims, of Great Burstead, Essex, and his wife Marie *(40). Christopher died in the epidemic aboard the *Mayflower* as it lay off Plymouth Bay, New England on 8 January 1621. Marie died a few months later. They had two manservants, John Langmore * and Solomon Prower *.

14. William Mullins *(40), formerly a shopkeeper of Dorking (B2), Surrey. He was accompanied by his wife, Alice * and children Priscilla (18) and Joseph * (6). After the first winter, the only survivor was Priscilla and, in time, she married John Alden, the cooper who boarded the *Mayflower* in Southampton. With the Mullins on board ship was a manservant named Robert Carter *.

15. **John Rigdale** *, formerly of London and his wife, **Alice** *. Both were early victims of the epidemic.

16. **Thomas Rogers** * (30+), a merchant, and son **Joseph** (12). After Thomas died, Joseph was eventually joined by the rest of the family in New England. He fathered six children and died at Eastham, New England in 1678.

17. **Captain Miles Standish** (36) and his wife, **Rose** *, who came from the Isle of Man. Captain Standish was to undertake security issues and defence of the Plimoth Plantation. After Rose's early death, Miles re-married and moved in 1632 to Duxbury, New England, named after the place where the Standish family seems to have originated.

18. **Edward Tilley** * (46), formerly a clothmaker of London, and his wife, **Ann Tilley** *. Also accompanying them were two young cousins – Humility Cooper (8) and Henry Sampson (6).

After the early deaths of Edward and Ann, Humility returned to England whilst Henry eventually married and had seven children. He died at Duxbury, New England in 1684.

19. **John Tilley** * (49), formerly a silk maker from London, and his wife **Bridget** *, whom he met in Holland. There was also their daughter, Elizabeth (14). John and Bridget suffered early deaths. Elizabeth married John Howland, formerly of London, and, on his death, another Pilgrim. Elizabeth died at Plymouth, New England in 1687.

20. **Thomas Tinker** * (39), a wood sawyer, his **wife** * and young **son** *. All died in the epidemic of 1621.

21. **John Turner** * (35), formerly a merchant, and two young **sons** *. All died early.

22. **William White** * (28), formerly a wool carder, his wife **Susannah** (26) and one son – **Resolved** (5). Another son, Peregrine, was born on arrival in Cape Cod harbour – the first of the Pilgrims to be born in the New World. After William's death, Susannah married Governor Edward Winslow. She died at Marshfield (F22), New England in 1680. Resolved married, fathered five children and died in Salem, Massachusetts in 1680. Peregrine eventually married, had two children and died at Marshfield in 1704. Also with the White family were two menservants – **William Holbeck** * and **Edward Thompson** *. Neither survived the epidemic.

23. Richard Warren (40), described as a merchant of London who had served in the Honourable Artillery Company of London in 1612. He travelled alone on the *Mayflower* and left his wife and five daughters behind for them to follow at a later date. This they did and two sons were born to them in New England. He died at Plymouth, New England in 1628.

24. **Edward Winslow** (25) and his wife, **Elizabeth** * (23). After Elizabeth's death, Edward married Susannah White. He also had charge of the fourth of the More children – Elinor * (8) who was to die in the epidemic. Edward was eventually to return to England to represent the interests of New England in Parliament.

There were also two menservants in the Winslow household – **George Soule** (21) and **Elias Story** * (42). The former later married and fathered eight children. He died at Duxbury, New England in 1680. The latter died in the epidemic in 1621.

* * *

Eventually, on 9 November, land was sighted. Instead of arriving, as originally planned, in that part of 'Virginia' to the north of the Hudson river, the Pilgrims found they were just off Cape Cod, about 450 miles (720 kilometres) further north. It looked a desolate place made worse by the fact that winter was beginning to take hold.

They had all had enough of life at sea. However, there was no sign of any existing settlement where they could be set down. The Elders of the Pilgrims conferred with Captain Jones about the best course of action. Perhaps they should head south and aim for a landing place around the Hudson? The entire coast was known already to English mariners. Captain John Smith had earlier explored it, including the area around Cape Cod. Jones's advice was to warn them of the dangers of pursuing such a course in extreme conditions. After establishing the ship's position, he decided they were off the northern tip of Cape Cod. He steered the *Mayflower* on a southerly course and for a few hours followed the coastline of the narrow spit of land which encloses the Bay of Cape Cod. Very soon they began to run into difficulties amidst shallow water, sandbanks and howling winds. There was no alternative but to head out into the open sea to escape danger. As soon as he was able, Captain Jones steered the ship in a northerly direction to the tip of Cape Cod and rounded it to find shelter within the bay. He soon came across a natural harbour close to the area now known as Provincetown (F17) and sailed into its confines. The surrounding area, with limited vegetation, seemed devoid of any sign of life.

When the *Mayflower* had set sail from Plymouth she carried 102 passengers. With three deaths and two births en route there were 101 when the ship arrived at Provincetown (F17).

Due to the change of plan by Captain Jones to land elsewhere, the frustration and anger of some of the Pilgrims began to boil over. One school of thought was that they should leave the ship and establish the new colony where they had arrived. Another was that they should wait patiently until reasonable weather conditions would allow them to proceed southwards via Pollock Rip, below Monomoy Island, and head towards the Hudson which was thought to be a better place to live. The arguments continued but with no satisfactory conclusion.

At that point, one of the senior Elders recalled the final letter written to them by John Robinson, their pastor in Holland. Amongst other sound advice, he had suggested they 'become a body politic using amongst yourselves civil government, and are not furnished with any persons of special eminency above the rest to be chosen by you into office of government. Let your wisdom and godliness appear, not only in choosing such persons as do entirely love, and will diligently promote, the common good; but also in yielding unto them all due honour and obedience in their lawful administrations.'

Taking heed of Robinson's words of wisdom, the Elders promptly called a meeting of all principal passengers and heads of households. Together, they drew up an agreement for each head of household to put his name to:

In y name of God, Amen. We, whose names are underwritten, the loyal subjects of our dread Soveraign Lord King James; by y grace of God, of Great Britaine, Franco and Ireland King; Defendor of the Faith; etc..

Haveing undertaken for y glorio of God, and advancements of y Christian faith and honour of our King and countrie, a voyage to plant y first colonie y northern parts of Virginia; do by these presents, solemnly and mutualy, in y presence of God and one of another, covenant and combine ourselves togeather into a Civil Body Politick, for our better ordering and preservation; and furtherance of y ends aforesaid:and by vertue hereof, to enact, constitute, and frame such just and equal laws, ordinances, acts, constitutions and offices. from time to time, as shall be thought most meete and convenient for y generall good of y Colonie; unto which, we promiso all due submission and obedience. In witnes whereof, we have hereunder subscribed our names at Cape Codd, 11 of November, in y year of y raigne of our Soveraign Lord King James of England, Franco and Ireland eighteenth and of Scotland y fiftio fourth. Anno Domini 1620.

This document became known as the Mayflower Compact and it was signed by 41 men. John Carver was elected as Governor of the new colony for the first twelve months.

Although they had originally planned to land in the vicinity of the Hudson or Connecticut, the Pilgrims took the decision to disregard the terms of their patent and settle in New England. So that was that!

One of the first tasks was for a group of men to explore the local terrain to try to establish if there were any signs of a settlement in the vicinity. There would have been a desperate need for fresh water and foodstuffs. Despite the bleak conditions which greeted them, the group would also have been anxious to set foot on land once again, for they had finally reached their destination – the New World. The Pilgrims knelt in prayer to thank the Lord for delivering them into their own 'Promised Land'. A new way of life was about to begin.

CHAPTER 9

New World – New Horizons

THE FOLLOWING DAY WAS the Sabbath and all attempts at exploration were postponed by the Pilgrims to allow them time for prayer and thanksgiving for their deliverance. However, they soon began to realise that the area around Provincetown would not provide sufficient shelter for a new settlement. Captain Jones was anxious that they decide either to find a suitable place to moor the ship – or be prepared to return to England! Consequently, on Wednesday 15 November, Captain Standish and a group of men set out from the Mayflower in a shallop (open boat) in order to explore the coastline.

* * *

The Pilgrim Monument in Provincetown is the tallest all-granite structure in the United States and commemorates the first landfall of the Pilgrim Fathers. It was erected in 1910 and includes an observation deck on top of the 252 foot structure (116 steps and 60 ramps) which allows sweeping views of the entire Cape. There is a small museum located near the base of the tower which houses a permanent collection of documents and artefacts, including a model of the *Mayflower*, and both the tower and museum are open to visitors during the tourist season. Today, Provincetown combines elements of a fishing village, artists' colony and resort.

* * *

With winter approaching, daylight was short and visibility was probably very limited for the Pilgrims and the land must have appeared desolate as they rowed along the water's edge. By all accounts, all they could see were stark, endless stretches of sand. On landing, the group proceeded to walk along the shoreline for about a mile to the north-east. Suddenly, they spotted a group of Indians with a dog approaching. When, in turn, the Indians saw the Pilgrims, they turned, ran off into the woodland, and disappeared. The place where the sighting took place is now known as First Encounter Beach (F15) near Eastham. That night, the men camped out, finding what shelter and warmth they could to keep them from exposure. Next day, they continued their exploration and eventually discovered fresh water at a place which is today known as Pilgrim Spring. It must have been almost too good to be true after all the saltwater they had endured during the voyage across the Atlantic.

Pushing onwards, they followed the tracks of the Indians to East Harbour Creek and continued along the coast until all signs of footprints petered out. Suddenly, they stumbled upon a clearing where there were a number of Indian graves filled with artefacts which they first examined and then replaced out of respect for the dead. There were also the remains of a campsite and little mounds of sand. On further investigation, they discovered that under these were baskets of corn which had been buried by the Indians. They also came across an old shack in which there was evidence that someone had lived there – perhaps a shipwrecked sailor. In the dwelling were some planks and a large kettle which they later used to carry corn. Nearby was an area where shoots of corn was actually sprouting and also in the vicinity were wild fruits, grapevines and walnut trees. These would all help provide food and a valuable lifeline for the Pilgrims. The corn was kept and later planted to provide crops for them in following years. Various implements which they discovered were further evidence of the place once having been some sort of Indian settlement. Today the location is known as Great Hollow.

That night, Captain Standish and his men built a bonfire to keep themselves warm and constructed a shelter to protect them from a heavy rainstorm. They could well have been in danger if the Indians had decided to attack. For this reason, armed with muskets, they mounted a guard in case of ambush. Fortunately, this did not happen and, next morning, saturated from the night's rain, the explorers set off to return to the ship. They trudged through undergrowth and along shifting sands until they finally reached the *Mayflower* in the evening. How glad they would be to be back on board to report their experiences and findings to the eagerly awaiting captain, crew and passengers. They had been in the New World exactly a week. Meanwhile, repairs to the shallop were necessary so there was a halt in further expeditions for a few days. Eventually, on the seventeenth day, the shallop was ready for use again.

Some 30 men, including Captain Jones, set off in two boats in a southerly direction to explore East Harbour's Pamet River. Unfortunately, the weather became so bad that they had to abandon the boats at Beach Point. The party continued on foot for another six miles. By the following day, the wind had dropped and this allowed them to continue their journey by boat. Edward Winslow and some others reached the foot of Old Tom's Hill, which was situated between two creeks of the Pamet River. This area proved fruitless as the channels were shallow and could only accommodate the smallest of vessels. Captain Jones took with him a smaller group to walk along the shore. As there had been an overnight snowstorm, the way proved difficult and dangerous as the men clambered over the icy terrain and slippery rocks. After some while the Captain began to tire, complained he was exhausted and insisted they stay put for another day. This pause gave some of the men the opportunity to hunt for game.

The next day, bearing in mind the treacherous conditions, they made a change of plan. Instead of continuing along the shoreline, they decided to try to re-discover the Indian settlement which they had stumbled across a few days' earlier. After several hours they found it. This time, they spotted an abandoned canoe which they used to cross the river to the place where they first discovered corn buried by the Indians. On arrival, they helped themselves to more supplies and also came upon a bottle of oil.

They decided to split into two groups. One, which included Captain Jones, would return to the *Mayflower* with fresh supplies. The other, consisting of eighteen men, would continue to explore. In the former party would be some of those who had found the going too tough and rigorous, bearing in mind that many had suffered seasickness and illness during the Atlantic crossing coupled with the extreme and changing weather conditions they had experienced since they had first dropped anchor.

Whilst the men had been away exploring, the womenfolk had not been idle and at last had been able to wash in clean water some of the clothing and other articles they had used on board ship. They would also have been delighted at the opportunity to use the water for their own personal bathing and hygiene. Despite having arrived, the ship was still the only place where everyone could live until such time as proper homes could be constructed. In the meanwhile, they had to put up with the continuing cramped conditions.

Captain Jones had promised the group of explorers that the shallop would return with tools to allow them to dig for further supplies of corn. They were hoping to come across an Indian village but only succeeded in finding a large mound which, on investigation, proved to be the grave of an Indian adult and a child, along with implements for embalming and a few personal effects. Meanwhile, the shallop returned with the tools and two men went ashore to look for the others. By chance, they came upon two rather odd dwellings – wigwams – which looked as if they had only just been abandoned. The two sailors, brandishing muskets, approached with caution only to find the dwellings were empty. They then made their way back to the shallop to report their findings. Others came to take a look and took away one or two items as souvenirs to show to the other passengers on board the *Mayflower*. Discussion then turned on whether this might be a suitable place to establish their settlement. There were mixed feelings as they weighed up the pros and cons of staying put around the Pamet River.

It was generally agreed that the area on the spit of land known as Cape Cod was in far too exposed a position. This meant they must continue their exploration to find somewhere suitable around the bay. A suggestion was then made by Robert Coppin, one of the pilots on the *Mayflower*, who had sailed in the area on an earlier occasion. He gave details of a headland on the western side of the Bay where he had landed previously during a fishing expedition – Manomet Bluff (F18). On that occasion, his party had lost their boat to Indians whilst they were exploring. In pursuit of the robbers, they came across an excellent harbour to the north. This had earlier been named as Plymouth by explorer, Captain John Smith, and it appeared on the map of New England which he made in 1614.

On Wednesday 6 December, the shallop was used for another exploration. On board were Captain Miles Standish, William Bradford, John Carver, Richard Clarke, Edward Doty, Stephen Hopkins, John Howland, John and Edward Tilley, Richard Warren and Edward Winslow. There were also three members of the crew and the ship's gunner. Slowly, the vessel sailed south along the Cape Cod peninsula opposite Truro, aiming for Billingsgate Point. They reached the area now known as Eastham (F14) in the evening. At this point, the Pilgrims spotted a group of Indians cutting up fish but decided not to approach them. Instead, they landed a cautious distance away to settle down for the night, lit a fire and built adequate protection in case of attack.

The next day the party split into two groups – one on foot and the other in the shallop to explore the Wellfleet Harbour area (F16). The day was uneventful. In the evening they were building a fire and barricade when a warning was given by one of the guards. He reported hearing a howling noise which they agreed must have been wolves. A few hours later, during breakfast, the same howling was heard again. This time, one of the men rushed in to announce that Indians were about to attack. They quickly grabbed their muskets as arrows were fired in their direction by about 40 attackers. Shots from the muskets soon dispersed the Indians. The men pursued them but their assailants were soon out of sight. In thankfulness to God, the Pilgrims knelt in prayer for another safe deliverance.

The weather began to deteriorate as they set off again in the shallop. Robert Coppin reiterated his earlier comments of knowing of a safe harbour and stated they were now very close to the site. As it happened, he turned out to have been mistaken and the shallop drifted in a howling gale. There was no alternative but to abandon the idea that night and find shelter on the nearest shore.

The storm dropped and the weather was much improved by morning. It was then that the Pilgrims realised they had landed on an isolated island now known as Clarke's Island and named after a later owner and not, according to popular tradition, after John Clarke, the first mate and pilot of the *Mayflower*. A brighter day gave them the chance to dry out and take stock. As the next day was the Sabbath, they stayed on and observed it in their usual way.

On Monday 11 December 1620 they took to the shallop again to further explore the coastline. Heading westwards across what is now known as Duxbury Bay they suddenly sailed into a large harbour which seemed to be the sort of place they had been looking for since their arrival. Perhaps their search for a suitable location was finally over?

Having moored the shallop in the vicinity of Plymouth Bay, the Pilgrims immediately set about scanning the area. They landed at a point between Captain's Hill and Plymouth Rock (F19) and soon discovered there were 'diverse cornfeilds and little runing brooks' which made them decide on that location. (Since that day 11 December has been celebrated each year as Forefathers' Day.)

The following day, the men returned to the *Mayflower* to announce their decision to the remaining crew and passengers. However, when they arrived on board, there was tragic news awaiting. They were told that, during their absence, Dorothy Bradford, wife of Elder William Bradford, had fallen overboard and drowned. There had been other deaths on the ship, mainly people weak from disease in the infected environment on board. These included James Chilton, the *Mayflower*'s oldest passenger, Edward Thompson and young Jasper Moore. They were buried on the coast at Provincetown where a stone commemorates their deaths.

Not all the Pilgrims were at first convinced that Plymouth would be a suitable place for a settlement and so a further exploration was made. The intention was to inspect the area to find the best site for the community and to further examine natural supplies of water, grain, fruit and other crops. The area was good for fishing with many species of marine life being found in the Bay.

There was plenty of woodland which would provide additional wood for use in building work, and there were fruit trees. Meanwhile, preparations were being made on board the *Mayflower* for the landing of the Pilgrims. This was a distance of 25 miles (31 kilometres) from where they had originally dropped anchor. On 15 December, Captain Jones steered his ship from the shallow waters of Provincetown harbour and headed westwards across Cape Cod Bay. By now, there must have been a strong element of relief, excitement and anticipation as the Pilgrims had already been in the region for nearly five weeks.

After manoeuvring to find a safe harbour, Captain Jones dropped anchor in Plymouth Bay where the boat was to be moored until the spring. Three days later, excited though exhausted, the Pilgrims went ashore at Plymouth Rock. According to tradition, the first female to jump ashore was Mary Chilton, a vivacious sixteen-year-old, whose father had died on board the *Mayflower* as it lay in Cape Cod harbour. Weeks later, she was also to lose her mother.

* * *

Plymouth Rock, a small piece of glacial deposit, has become a shrine for millions of visitors. It has not always been known as an historic site and was actually identified in 1741 as the place where the Pilgrim Fathers set foot upon their arrival by Elder Thomas Faunce. He was a *Mayflower* descendant and third ruling elder of the Plymouth Church. In the same year, the town of Plymouth announced plans to erect a wharf in its harbour built so as to ensure the Rock was not hidden by the new development. In 1774, an attempt was made to move the Rock to a more public place during which process it split into two pieces. The lower was left where it was whilst the top half was transported to Town Square. It was again moved in 1834 to Pilgrim Hall which had been founded in 1820 to commemorate the bi-centenary of the Pilgrims' landing. 46 years later, the Rock was put back together in the harbour area where it was to lie under a monumental canopy until 1920. At the Tercentenary of the Pilgrims, the waterfront was re-developed again so as to place the rock on the edge

Plymouth Rock, New England

of the seashore, giving it a more natural appearance. It is protected by an elaborate portico.

* * *

The general concensus of opinion was that the plantation should be established on high ground to provide a good vantage point. An area to the north of the Town Brook had already been cleared and planted with corn. South of the brook were further cornfields whilst on the north-western side was an area of rising ground – known as Burial Hill – providing extensive views across to Cape Cod.

There was much to be done before work could start on building the settlement which they were to name New Plimoth Plantation. The word 'New' was dropped at a later date. For a start, sites for dwellings would have to be cleared, foundations laid, building materials and provisions unloaded from the Mayflower, wood to be gathered and food organised for the Pilgrims. However, the leading Pilgrims were satisfied with the location.

Progress was constantly hindered by bad weather which delayed the Pilgrims in getting on with the work of building homes for their families. There were two more deaths in quick succession when Richard Britteridge died and Mary Allerton was delivered of a still-born son. It was not until Christmas Day that a start was made on building the first houses. The Pilgrims did not celebrate Christmas as they considered it a pagan festival so they worked on as usual. With an improvement in the weather, all available men-folk were required to give a hand with the rough timber work to provide building materials. By the end of the day, tired from their labours, most of the men returned to the *Mayflower*. Others stayed on shore to guard their tools and supplies and the work they had already completed. Unfortunately, the weather worsened again and it was impossible for the shore party to make contact with those on board ship. It was not until three days later that there was some improvement in conditions, sufficient to allow the Pilgrims to continue their work.

One of their first priorities was to construct a wooden stock-ade or fort on the hilltop known as Burial Hill in order to defend the community from attack. A street of dwellings was built on either side of what is now known as Leyden Street in Plymouth. Plots were measured according to the number of people in each household and the Pilgrims drew lots for the best position of respective sites. An early requirement was for a 'common house' which could be used for storage of the tools and provisions previously kept on board ship. Work on this building was completed on 9 January 1621, only for a serious fire to break out five days later. The thatched roof was completely destroyed and although an icy downpour continued throughout the day, no effort was made to repair it. For it was the Sabbath day.

By now the hardships of the Atlantic crossing and continuing bad weather were really beginning to take their toll. Both Governor Carver and William Bradford were numbered amongst the sick whilst William Brewster and Captain Standish toiled relentlessly with surgeon, Doctor Samuel Fuller, to attend those who had fallen ill. Diggory Priest died soon after Richard Britteridge. The ship's Treasurer, Christopher Martin, Solomon Prower, John Langemore and Rose Standish also died before the end of January.

This was the start of the epidemic. Many must surely have questioned their wisdom in taking part in such a high risk venture in the first place. But they could only stand by and watch their loved ones slip away from them one by one. Yet the Pilgrims still had great faith. They were convinced it was the Lord's will and that He would carry them through, whatever the future might hold.

One of the worst storms they experienced took place on Sunday 4 February when the *Mayflower* almost capsized as most of the stores had by then been removed to the now-repaired 'common house'. By the middle of the month, sickness amongst crew and passengers was rife. As deaths occurred, bodies of the settlers were buried by night in ground which is now named Cole's Hill after a later proprietor. As a precaution, the earth was smoothed over after each burial in order not to alert the Indians as to how many survivors were still in the colony. Occasionally, they had glimpses of Indians and, on one occasion, discovered that some of their tools had been stolen. In order to defend themselves, members of the company were armed with muskets and Captain Standish was put in charge of all security arrangements.

Then the unexpected happened.

Turning of the Tide

A LONE INDIAN WAS seen approaching the colony and walked up to the settlers. To their surprise, he spoke in broken English and stated his name was Samoset and that he came from Pemaquid Point, situated at what is now called Bristol in the state of Maine. It was there that he had earlier met and talked with English seafarers who taught him a few words of their language. He appeared to be well informed about the area and local Indian tribes. The man went on to explain to the settlers that, four years earlier, the Indians had abandoned Patuxet – their own name for the area known as New Plymouth – due to a plague when all the inhabitants died. He also informed them of the Indians' suspicion of any settlers since earlier explorers, under Sir Fernando Gorges and captained by Thomas Hunt, had deceived them by capturing 27 of their people and shipping them to Spain to be sold as slaves.

Samoset said the name of the local chief was Massasoit and that another Indian called Squanto could speak English far better than he could himself. Squanto was one of the Indians originally seized by Captain Hunt and taken to Spain. However, he managed to escape whilst the ship was close to England and eventually made his way to London where he found a post with a London merchant in Cornhill and learned something of the English language. Eventually, he found a passage back to America with a French sea captain but managed to escape once again and returned to his own people. It was quite a remarkable story.

If only Samoset could be trusted? They gave him presents of a bracelet, ring and knife and, in response, he told them he would, on their behalf, help them set up a trade in animal furs to provide them with the means of acquiring much needed food and other provisions. At last, it appeared the tide was beginning to turn in the Pilgrims' favour.

Samoset kept his promise and came back with five Indians who not only returned the stolen tools but also brought deer and beaver skins. It was unfortunate that the day was the Sabbath and, apart from Samoset, the Indians were told to return with the furs another day. They did not come back and Samoset went off in search of them.

When he re-appeared, he was accompanied by 60 Indians and their chief, Massasoit, and his brother. Squanto, the English-speaker, was also present. Edward Winslow, clad in armour, stepped forward to greet them and presented Massasoit with a couple of knives, some trinkets and food. In turn, with Squanto as interpreter, he stated he wanted to start trading with the Pilgrims and it was arranged that Massasoit and his tribesmen would accompany Winslow to meet Governor John Carver. At the meeting, the Indians were received with courtesy and there was much bowing to one another. It was a successful encounter and resulted in a seven-point agreement being drawn up between the Pilgrims and the Indians. This proclaimed that no Indian should harm a settler in any way; if this happened the culprit should be sent to Plimoth Plantation for punishment; any stolen goods from either side should be returned or replaced; each side would come to the aid of the other in times of attack; any of Massasoit's men visiting the Plantation should arrive unarmed; Massasoit would inform other neighbouring tribes about the proposals in the agreement; and, finally, King James would recognise Massasoit as a friend and ally of England. The ice was broken.

Squanto proved to be a saviour to the settlers and they formed a close friendship with him. He was able to help the Pilgrims in so many ways as to how they should establish the settlement. He guided them around the Cape Cod Bay region on a number of expeditions, taught them where and how to fish, where to plant corn and how it should be fertilised. The man was a Godsend.

As winter turned to spring, the loss of members of the settlement continued. The settlers pulled together to comfort one another and ensure their survival. However, in April, Governor John Carver became ill whilst working in the cornfields and died

Plimoth Plantation

shortly afterwards. He was deeply mourned though, by then, the settlers must have become more hardened in the face of death. In his place, William Bradford was elected as the new head of the colony with Isaac Allerton as his Assistant.

The epidemic had also taken its toll on the crew of the *Mayflower* which had been reduced by half. Captain Jones had been anxious to to set out on the return journey but had to postpone this whilst the ship was being used for the storage of provisions and until his crew were in a better shape healthwise. It is interesting to note that, despite their hardships, not one of the Pilgrims elected to return to their homeland.

Eventually the *Mayflower* set sail on 5 April 1621, arriving in England on 6 May, a much swifter passage than its outward voyage to the New World due to it carrying a much lighter load and having more specific directions. The ship was refitted before moving to its regular moorings at Rotherhithe. Over the following months, the *Mayflower* made one or two trading voyages to France and other European countries, then was left lying and allowed to rot. In 1624, nearing dereliction, the *Mayflower* was valued at just over £138. It was broken up at Rotherhithe later that year. Captain Jones did not live long. Within twelve months of his return to England he died and was buried at St. Mary's Church, Rotherhithe, on 5 March 1622.

In 1955, a reconstruction of the *Mayflower* took place at Upham's Yard at Brixham (A7). The replica set sail from Plymouth in 1957 on a passage to re-enact that eventful voyage of 1620. *Mayflower II* did, in fact, take thirteen days less than the original. Since that time it has been moored at the State Pier in the harbour at Plymouth, Massachusetts, where it has become a major visitor attraction. It is staffed by costumed 'Pilgrims' who relate to visitors the tale of their journey across the Atlantic to the New World.

* * *

In modern-day Plymouth there is still much to see which recalls the rich heritage of the days of the Pilgrim Fathers and Plimoth Colony. As we stroll along the Waterfront, we are surrounded by reminders of the past. As well as *Mayflower II* and Plymouth Rock under its portico on the beach by Water Street, other attractions include the Mayflower Society House, Pilgrim Hall Museum and the National Forefathers' Monument in Allerton Street which honours the Pilgrims and their small colony. The large monument was a prototype for the Statue of Liberty. The essence of New Plymouth's history is captured in the numerous museums and historic houses which are open during the tourist season.

The splendid building occupied by the Mayflower Society is in Winslow Street and was built during the colonial period and later enlarged. The house is a graceful mixture of Colonial and Victorian architecture and has a white wooden exterior. The interior contains a flying stairway and on display are antiques including a rare set of biblical fireplace tiles in the drawing room. The Society's activities and records involve many countries across the world wherever there is a connection or interest in the *Mayflower* and descendants of those early pioneers who founded the New World.

Pilgrim Hall Museum is another memorial to the Pilgrims and Plimoth Colony and is a granite structure designed by Alexander

Parris. The displays include the most complete collection of authentic Pilgrim possessions, with original furniture and rare examples of 17th-century shipbuilding, household goods, weapons and books. Artefacts include chairs owned by Governors Carver and Bradford; the cradle of Peregrine White who was born on the *Mayflower*; the sword of Miles Standish and a sampler made by his daughter, Lora Standish. You can also see Bibles belonging to John Alden and Governor Bradford. Displays in the museum relate the story of the Pilgrim Fathers and other settlers who followed them. It is a must for everyone with an interest in the subject.

Not far from the waterfront is Plymouth National Wax Museum, located on Cole's Hill. It contains numerous life-size dioramas which, enhanced by realistic soundtracks, depict the Pilgrim story from Scrooby and the flight to Holland in 1607 to the first Thanksgiving celebration of 1621. Fronting the museum is a statue of the chief, Massasoit, who was instrumental of helping the Pilgrims in so many ways during their early days at Plimoth Colony.

Other places worth seeing, a number within a short walking distance of the Waterfront, include the Jenney Grist Mill, a faithful replica of a 1636 Pilgrim watermill for grinding corn, wheat and rye; Spooner House, an 18th-century residence on Water Street; Richard Sparrow House, built in 1642 and the oldest surviving house in Plymouth; Jabez Howland House, the only house still standing where Pilgrims are known to have lived; and the Old Court House in Town Square, built in 1749 and claimed to be the oldest surviving wooden courthouse in America. Quite close to the Old Court House is Burial Hill, where the old cemetery contains gravestones which date back to the time of Plimoth Colony. The Town Brook, near where the Pilgrims built their first settlement, still wends its way through the wooded parkland of Brewster Gardens on its way to meet the sea.

Like its counterpart in Devon, Plymouth is a popular maritime centre; it organises regular boat trips to places such as Provincetown, Cape Cod Canal, Boston Harbour Islands and the

islands of Nantucket (F7) and Martha's Vineyard, an island originally discovered by Bartholomew Gosnold in 1602. Plymouth is
also a good base for whale-watching trips in one of the few areas
where great whales can be seen on a regular basis. Expert marine
biologists are on board to identify and describe the whales and
birds to be spotted during the cruises. The region's great heydays
of whaling are recalled in Herman Melville's famous novel *Moby
Dick*, a book which was later filmed.

Perhaps the most popular and colourful attraction in the area
is Plimoth Plantation which is situated about three miles (five kilometres) south of Plymouth centre, taking Route 3 out of the town.
This living history museum is a faithful reconstruction of the original settlement founded by the Pilgrims as it would have appeared
in 1627. Buildings are peopled by costumed guides who explain
what life was really like during that era. Actors play the roles of
original Pilgrims and re-enact the roles of specific early Separatists
who came to settle. They speak in Jacobean English and their
activities include gardening, cookery, harvesting and even how to
build a timber-framed house. Adjoining the village is
Hobbamock's Homesite where the culture of this native American
Indian group is demonstrated by native interpreters who speak
from a contemporary point of view about the experiences of their
ancestors as well as the life of the Wampanoag native Americans
of today. They demonstrate how to raise crops, dry food, weave
and other occupations.

At the entrance to the village is a fort which gives a good vantage point over the whole location with its neat rows of thatched-
roof cottages similar to those which would have been occupied by
the early inhabitants. Plimoth Plantation transports the visitor
back to the 17th century and provides a wonderful time capsule
for study or just an enjoyable and interesting experience.

* * *

As the summer of 1621 approached in Plimoth Colony, with
much help from Squanto, food became more plentiful and life
began to take on some form of normality. For a start, there was
more personal comfort when houses and other buildings were

completed. Stocks of furs kept the settlers warm and they were also becoming more proficient at planting and tending crops. There was a joyous occasion in the colony on 12 May when widower, Edward Winslow, married widow, Susanna White. The ceremony was a civil one at which the new Governor, William Bradford, officiated. Three sons were born to the couple of which two died in infancy. There are, however, many living descendants of the surviving son, Josiah.

By this time the Indians were regular visitors to the colony, sometimes making a nuisance of themselves by taking food belonging to the settlers. In a diplomatic effort to settle the matter, Edward Winslow and Stephen Hopkins set out with Squanto to meet Massasoit at his main camp situated some 40 miles (64 kilometres) distant. It was a cordial meeting at which the chief promised his people would trouble the settlers no more.

One day in July, the nine-year-old son of John Billington ran off into the woods just south of Plimoth Colony and disappeared. Despite an intensive search, he was nowhere to be found. Had he been captured by Indians? Despite the general dislike of the Billington family because of their anti-social behaviour, the Pilgrims would not abandon the boy. Bradford issued instructions that ten of his men along with Squanto and another Indian should arm themselves and search the coastline in the shallop. Due to bad weather, they decided to drop anchor overnight south of Cape Cod Bay near the present Barnstaple. Next day, they spotted Indians on the shoreline and approached them.

The Indians knew of the whereabouts of the young boy. He had been found wandering by one of them who had taken care of him and he was safe at Nauset – now known as Eastham. The search party was invited by the Cummaquid tribe to share a meal with them where they met the chief, Iyanough. Unfortunately, they were challenged by an old Indian woman who, they discovered, had had three sons captured by Captain Hunt at the same time as Squanto and taken to Spain as slaves. Squanto was very sympathetic to the woman's anguish.

This did not augur well. The statement by the old lady would have angered the Indians. In retaliation for the kidnappings it appeared that they had already taken revenge by murdering three Englishmen. It would therefore be unwise to linger in the Indian camp any longer. In haste, they returned to the shallop and made for Nauset where Squanto and Tokamahamon were delegated to go ashore to make enquiries about the young boy.

No sooner had they gone than a crowd of Indians appeared on the beach and splashed into the water to surround the boat. It looked like an ambush but the settlers were able to hold their own. Two Indians were invited to talk, and one was the man whose corn had been taken by the settlers when they first arrived in the area. They gladly agreed to recompense him for his loss and suggested he come to reclaim it in person from Plimoth Plantation. He agreed to this. In the evening, the chief of the Nauset tribe, Aspinet, appeared on the beach along with members of his tribe, and with them was the Billington boy whom one of them placed on board the shallop. In turn, the Pilgrims presented Aspinet with a knife along with a gift for the Indian who had found and taken care of the child. The settlers breathed a sigh of relief as they set sail back to New Plymouth.

By September the Pilgrims had gathered in the harvest and held their first Thanksgiving. Since 1863, Thanksgiving Day has been celebrated in North America as a national holiday – on the fourth Thursday of November in the USA and the second Monday of October in Canada. As a token of their appreciation for the help they received from the Indians, they invited Massasoit and 90 of his braves and their squaws as their honoured guests to join them at a feast. As a contribution, the Indians brought five deer which they had slaughtered for the occasion. However, after the feast, the Pilgrims found themselves short of food for the winter months which could cause major problems if stocks were not replenished in time.

Due to the good rapport which had been established by the English settlers with the Indians around Cape Cod Bay, Governor Bradford decided to try and make contact with the Massachusett tribe who lived around Boston Bay. It was rumoured that English settlers were under threat from this tribe. A ten-strong party of men, led by Captain Standish and accompanied by Squanto and two other Indians, set out northwards in the shallop to explore Massachusetts Bay. In so doing, they named various places. The long spit of land at the south end of the bay was named Port Allerton, the islands at the entrance were named Brewster and, in tribute to their Indian friend, a headland was named Squantum. They finally landed in a bay that would soon become known as Boston Harbour (F25) where they met a chief who warned them of the dangers of the Tarentine tribe and their thieving ways. This tribe inhabited the banks of the Penobscot River in Maine to the north. They were also warned to be cautious of Squaw Sachem, Queen of the Massachusett tribe, who lived on the northern side of Boston Bay.

Captain Standish decided to tackle the problem head on and they sailed northwards along the coast to seek out Squaw Sachem. They threaded their way through the various islands from what is today known as Quincy (F24) to Charlestown, and landed at a deserted beach. Captain Standish sent Squanto to take a look around the area but he returned without having found anyone. The following day the group proceeded inland, leaving two men to guard the shallop.

They first came across a small settlement and, further on, a wooden fortification on a hilltop. They then found the women of the tribe, clad in furs, gathering corn. On spotting the settlers arriving in the shallop, the menfolk had hurriedly gathered their belongings and moved off. The frightened women pointed out the location of their settlement. Wigwams had already been dismantled and tribesmen scattered in various directions. Squanto directed one of the women to search for the men and request they meet with him and the rest of the group. It was, however, some time before a terrified warrior appeared, only to inform them that Squaw Sachem was miles away.

Squanto tried to persuade the English settlers to help themselves to the animal skins worn by the women, but they refused. The women followed the group back to the shallop where they unexpectedly removed their furs and offered them in exchange for trinkets. Finally, the settlers set off for the Plimoth Colony, a few miles to the south. It had been an interesting expedition.

* * *

In England, negotiations were taking place by the London Virginia Company. It appeared that the charter given by the Company to the *Mayflower* Pilgrims did not extend as far north as their proposed destination around the River Hudson. This was creating a problem for the Company. Furthermore, the second of the two Virginia Companies had been replaced by a Council of New England. This made it necessary for the London Company of Adventurers, sponsors of the *Mayflower*, to apply to this Council for a new charter in order to legalise the standing of the Pilgrims already in New Plymouth. This was granted on 1 June 1621.

Robert Cushman of Canterbury, one of the original negotiators for the *Mayflower* for the first crossing of Pilgrims in 1620, then began transactions for a second party to join their brethren in the New World. There would soon be a new influx of Pilgrims arriving in New England. Governor Bradford knew nothing about it and it was to create untold problems.

CHAPTER 11

The Floodgates are Opened

IN JULY 1621, the *Fortune* set sail from England conveying a second group of Pilgrims to join the original party already in Plimoth Plantation. Thirty-five passengers travelled in the small ship of 55 tons which had been chartered by Robert Cushman. Thus began the second stage of the Pilgrim story.

Cushman headed the party of emigrants along with his fourteen-year-old son, Thomas. There were also other Separatists who had journeyed from Leiden and close relatives of a few people who had already settled in New England. Amongst these was Jonathan Brewster, eldest son of Elder William Brewster, and John Winslow, brother of Elder Edward Winslow. There was also the sixteen year-old boy, Phillipe de la Noye, once a member of the Walloon community in Leiden. He later changed his surname from de la Noye to Delano and was the ancestor of two American presidents (as mentioned earlier in Chapter 5).

Others in the party included John Adams, a carpenter; William Bassett, gunsmith and metal worker; William Wright, leather dresser; Stephen Deane, miller; and Robert Hicks and Clement Briggs, fellmongers. Each of these trades was to be useful when they joined the colony. Captain of the *Fortune* was Thomas Barton, who reported that, on first sighting the deserted Cape Cod, many passengers had grave doubts about their future if there was nobody left in the colony to receive them.

Those already settled had not had any contact with England since they first arrived. Fourteen months had now elapsed. A major problem was that Robert Cushman had not made arrangements for extra food and provisions. Consequently, the passengers were hungry by the time they reached the New World. Stocks were low in Plimoth Plantation due in part to the Thanksgiving celebrations to which the Governor had earlier invited the Indians.

The sight of a ship on the horizon must have thrown members of the colony into a panic as they pondered who it might bring. There was always the possibility of attack by the French, Spanish or others, so it was with great caution that they made their way down to the shore to investigate. Imagine their surprise and delight to discover the *Fortune* had brought a number of friends and close relatives as well as others who were looking to settle in the New World. With them came letters from loved ones in both Leiden and London. However, when the Pilgrims found the ship was devoid of provisions, they realised they had a major problem on their hands. How were they to feed everyone? It was to lead to near-starvation for a great number. Robert Cushman had to take the blame for this and realised he had made a serious error. He had proved unpopular with the Pilgrims even before they left England through his inconsistent attitude and activities over the agreement for the *Mayflower* voyage. On the positive side, the number of extra hands and skilled tradesmen would assist in the construction work on the colony.

Cushman was the bearer of bad tidings in the form of a letter from Thomas Weston who had addressed it to the late Governor, John Carver, not knowing of his death. It was therefore passed to Governor Bradford to read. Weston complained bitterly about the long delay of the *Mayflower*'s return to England, and the fact there was no cargo on board for trading purposes. After all, the Merchant Adventurers had been keen to see a return on their original investment. Weston stated in his letter that he had avoided reporting to the Adventurers the details of the Pilgrims' earlier disputes prior to leaving for the New World, insisting that they copy out the terms of the agreement and other stipulations. Had they known of these disputes, the Adventurers would not have funded the project in the first place.

Weston continued by informing the Pilgrims of the new agreement from the Council of New England which had been drawn up for the Adventurers under the name of John Pierce. It allocated one hundred acres of land to each colonist and they were to be given the freedom to fish and transact business. In addition, 1,500 acres were to be allocated to each Adventurer. It also stated that after seven years a comprehensive survey would be made and the charter replaced by a new document setting out precise boundaries and governing rights. In the meantime all 'laws made by the undertakers, planters, and their associates would be considered legal'. This of course meant that the Pilgrims' occupation of Plimoth Plantation was now legal and above board.

In response, Governor Bradford wrote a diplomatic letter to Thomas Weston, informing him of the death of Governor Carver and going on to explain the hardships they had had to endure such as the conditions during the voyage and the dreadful weather, the illness and epidemic and their lack of proper food and shelter. He also stated that nearly half their community had already died and emphasised the constant danger they were under by threat of invasion from Indians and other Europeans.

Robert Cushman was to return to England in the *Fortune* and hand over the Governor's letter to Weston upon arrival. Perhaps then he might have some understanding of their predicament? In the absence of his father, young Thomas Cushman was made a ward of Governor Bradford until such time as Robert returned. Also on board for the return journey was a cargo of various items including beaver skins, timber and laurel which the Pilgrims had accumulated. These the Adventurers would sell at a profit.

Before he left, Robert Cushman preached a sermon to a full and enthusiastic congregation of Pilgrims in the community house. In the main, his simple message to them was that they should each place the interests of the community above their own. On 11 December 1621, the *Fortune* set sail on the return journey with Cushman on board. With him went various accounts of the Pilgrims' activities in the colony and a letter from Governor Bradford addressed to the Adventurers and the parent Separatist church in Leiden. In addition, Edward Winslow wrote letters to colleagues in England which have been preserved and give an authoritative account of the life and experiences of the Pilgrim Fathers during their early days in the New World. Cushman took these to a London printer who published the writings – now known as *Mourt's Relation (or Journal)* of the English Plantation settled at Plymouth by 'certain English adventurers both merchants and others'. Likewise, the journal of Governor William Bradford was published under the title of *Of Plimoth Plantation* and gives a vivid account of the same period and also includes letters by John Robinson, Robert Cushman and Thomas Weston.

Although the *Fortune* managed to reach the English Channel safely, it was ambushed by a pirate ship from France and escorted to Brittany where the cargo was stolen along with all other items considered of value. The passengers and crew were then released and allowed to proceed to London where they arrived on 17 February 1622. Fortunately, the French were not interested in the various reports carried by Cushman so he was able to retrieve official documents and the letter to Weston. In addition, the diary notes and manuscripts written by Edward Winslow and William Bradford were thankfully saved for posterity.

* * *

It soon came to the attention of the Indians that more settlers had arrived at Plimoth Plantation and this disturbed them. The Naragansett tribe were angry and sent one of their people to the colony. He threw in front of the settlers a set of arrows wrapped in a snakeskin. Squanto explained to the Pilgrims that this was a threat and advised William Bradford to return the snakeskin filled with gunpowder. With it went a message stating that if the Indians wanted war, the settlers were ready for them and, as they had done no harm to the Indians in the past, all had a clear conscience.

When he received the response, the chief was afraid and, for the time being, no action was taken. In the meanwhile, the Pilgrims set about building a stout fence around the perimeter of the plantation in order to withstand attack. They also mounted a guard consisting of four squadrons of men, including some of the new settlers who had arrived on the *Fortune*.

However, the Pilgrims were short of food and skins for trading so the Governor ordered an expedition to improve the situation. Prior to their leaving, word was received that the Narragansett and Massachusett tribes were planning to curtail

First Thanksgiving, September 1621

Captain Standish's expeditions from New Plimoth, and also, when they left in the shallop, an attack would be mounted on the colony whilst manpower was short. Defiantly, the settlers set off for Boston Bay. When they reached Gurnet Point (F20), a relative of Squanto was spotted on the shore. He had been wounded by the Narragansetts for attempting to put them off raiding Plimoth Plantation and stated that Squanto was aiming to cause trouble between the various tribes. The Pilgrims returned to their settlement at once.

An enquiry was instigated by Governor Bradford and it came to light that Squanto had been doing his best to play a prominent role with the Pilgrims as well as position himself as a negotiator between warring tribes. He became over-conceited and began to accept bribes. This was bad news for the settlers as they had trusted Squanto who had always proved their useful ally and acted as their interpreter. Messages were therefore sent from the English settlers to local tribes stating they were only interested in making peace. In future, the Indians should disregard any communication brought by Squanto. In turn, Squanto was severely reprimanded by the Governor for his disloyalty. Massasoit, angry at Squanto's behaviour, demanded he be sent back to him for execution. Fortunately for Squanto, no action was taken by Bradford.

Another ship appeared in New Plymouth Bay in April 1622. It was from England – a fishing boat bound for the fishing grounds off the coast of Maine. When it had dropped anchor in the bay, a shallop was launched with seven men on board. They were met by Governor Bradford who conducted them to the community house for interrogation.

It appeared that the fishing boat had been commissioned by Thomas Weston who had sent a letter to the Governor informing him he was no longer dealing with the Company of Adventurers. In consequence, they were unwilling to transport any further Pilgrims from Leiden. Neither were the Separatists themselves in a position to finance another voyage. Nevertheless, Weston himself was looking to found a colony near Boston Bay and it appeared that the seven men who came ashore were further settlers arriving to start a new life in the colonies.

The letter from Weston was not the only document they brought. There was a message from John Huddleston, captain of another fishing boat which they had come across. He warned that 350 newcomers in Virginia had been massacred by Indians. This was bad news for the Pilgrims and they worried lest the incident might have a 'snowballing' effect amongst the Indians.

With seven more mouths to feed, the number in Plimoth Plantation now totalled 85. Food was fast running out as the new arrivals had neither brought provisions ashore nor were there any stocks on board ship other than enough for the crew for the return journey to England. In a desperate attempt to improve the situation, Edward Winslow set out in the shallop to catch up with the recently departed boat which by then had left New Plymouth Bay. On locating it, the captain could not help him. Eventually, Winslow found other fishing boats around the Monhegan area off the coast of Maine. The captains were sympathetic but could offer very little assistance as they only carried sufficient stocks for their own needs. Winslow returned to the colony frustrated. The only way they could survive was to eat wild fruits, game, the remaining crops, fish and any shellfish they could gather from nearby shores. The situation had now become desperate.

Then two more of Weston's ships sailed into the Bay in June 1622. Between them, the 100-ton *Charity* and the 30-ton *Swan* brought 60 further settlers, a number of whom were sick when they arrived. The newcomers proved to be a rather hostile, ill-mannered group who informed Governor Bradford that Weston had sent them to New Plymouth until a suitable location was found for them to establish a colony of their own around the Boston Bay area. Letters they brought from Weston, Robert Cushman and John Pierce of the Company of Adventurers confirmed the arrogance and brashness of the new arrivals, warning the Pilgrims to be wary of them and their loose-living ways.

Despite the problems, the Pilgrims did their best to make them feel welcome. They gave them food and made accommodation available in their own homes. They also helped tend the sick. After all, they felt it was their Christian duty. The ungrateful new arrivals repaid them by giving little assistance, refusing to take part in building work, tormenting the womenfolk and constantly stealing food and materials from the Pilgrims. The Pilgrims still 'turned the other cheek' in an effort to teach them Christian principles and about life in a new settlement.

It must have been a great relief to Governor Bradford and his community when news arrived that a suitable site had been found for the newcomers at a place called Wessagusset on the south side of Boston Bay which is today known as Weymouth. They departed in the *Swan*. The *Charity* then sailed on to Virginia with a number of passengers who were destined to settle there.

Word soon arrived that the new settlers at Wessagusset had created a lot of trouble with the Indians. This news would not have pleased the Governor who would now have to be doubly cautious of an Indian attack on his own colony. Work began in earnest to complete the fort and surrounding fences at Plimoth Plantation as well as strengthening the guard.

The harvest of 1622 had been poor. They would have to obtain corn from the Indians by the usual method of bartering with trinkets and other commodities. Unfortunately, they had little to trade. They would have to find some other means of obtaining sustenance. With their great faith in Jesus Christ, they knew that 'the Good Lord would provide!'

And so He did. This was by way of another ship returning to England from Virginia, the 60-ton *Discovery*, appearing in New Plymouth Bay. It had been commissioned by the Virginia Company and had on board a large stock of beads and knives which the captain was prepared to sell. Governor Bradford was involved in negotiations, giving beaver furs in exchange for the goods. The captain drove a hard bargain but the Pilgrims were in no position to refuse. At last, they had something to offer to the Indians in exchange for corn and furs.

Returning to England as a passenger on the *Discovery* was a man named John Pory, former secretary to the Governor of Virginia and a graduate of Caius College, Cambridge. He was obviously very impressed with the way of life in the plantation and how the Plimoth colony had been organised, and on his arrival back on English soil, he spoke in glowing terms of what the Pilgrim Fathers had achieved in New England.

In September 1622, the *Charity* reached Boston Bay on its return from Virginia. It brought a number of supplies for Weston's settlers at Wessagusset before leaving for England. The *Swan* and its shallop had been left for use by the new colonists. However, lacking the expertise of the Pilgrim leaders, the two Joint-Governors, John Sanders and Richard Green, were unable to make proper arrangements for the running or control of the new colony. They also soon discovered their foodstocks were running low.

When they heard that William Bradford of Plimoth Plantation had been successful in doing business with the Indians, Green asked the Pilgrims if he could borrow provisions from them. In return, he invited Governor Bradford to accompany him and other Boston settlers on a joint expedition to look for new supplies on the *Swan*. The newcomers would accompany the Pilgrims around Cape Cod Bay with the assurance they would reimburse anything they owed at a later date. The Governor agreed to the request and, jointly, they decided they would explore the southern coast. Winslow seconded Squanto to act as guide under the leadership of Richard Green. However, prior to the departure date, Green died and Miles Standish stepped in as leader of the expedition. Soon after departure, Standish was also taken ill and eventually was replaced by Bradford.

The voyage was not easy and the ship encountered a number of problems. It was soon driven back by bad weather and they came across dangerous currents near Cape Cod. Further difficulties were experienced in locating the Indians who, as so often the case, had gone into hiding. The Governor suggested they put into Manamoyick Bay, close to the present-day town of Chatham (F13). Eventually, Squanto made contact with the Indians and assured them the white men meant no harm. After some bartering, they agreed to let Bradford and his party have beans and eight hogsheads of corn.

After the transaction was concluded, Squanto became seriously ill and showed signs of a fever. He asked the Governor and his colleagues to pray for him that 'he might go to the Englishmen's God in Heaven'. Two days later he died. Squanto was greatly mourned by the Pilgrims because his help to them had been inestimable. They could not, in fact, have survived without him. Despite his earlier double-dealing for which he had begged the Governor's forgiveness, he would be sorely missed by everyone in the colony.

In the meanwhile, a second expedition was being led by John Sanders of the Wessagusset colony to meet the Massachusett tribe with a view to trading with them. The new colonists soon upset the Indians. Consequently, they had to pay dearly for their corn. On their return, Bradford warned them of the dire consequences if they continued to goad the local Indians, and it was agreed that the *Swan* be put under the charge of Governor Bradford whenever the Pilgrims wished to return to the Cape Cod region in an effort to locate new supplies.

Several more attempts were made in the *Swan* to obtain supplies. Eventually, the ship sailed into New Plymouth Bay with goods and then headed northwards to deliver the share for the Boston Bay settlers. Still unhappy with the amount of foodstocks in the colony, William Bradford organised two further expeditions – one to Manomet (Sandwich (F10)) and the other to Nameschet (Middleborough (F9)) where supplies of corn were obtained to help the Pilgrims through another winter. 'The Good Lord was providing.'

The food situation in Weston's colony at Wessagusset did not improve, and in order to obtain provisions, some of the settlers had taken desperate measures such as bartering with their clothes and even working as servants to the Indians. Again, in despair, they appealed to Governor Bradford for help. A letter was sent back refusing this. At some time in the future, a representative from the Court of King James would be sent from England to report on the progress and activities of English settlers in the new colonies. The Governor warned his counterpart at Wessagusset that when the day of reckoning finally arrived, he would be held personally responsible for any actions taken by his men.

News was received that Massasoit was ill and near to death. At the same time, information reached the Plantation that a Dutch ship had run aground at Sowans in Pokanoket (Warren in Bristol (F3), Rhode Island). This was where Massasoit had his principal residence. Bearing in mind the friendship he had shown to the Pilgrims, Elder Edward Winslow was delegated to visit the Chief to convey the good wishes of his community and take along any medicines which might be of help. At the same time, he also hoped to make contact with the Dutch ship. Winslow was accompanied by the Indian interpreter, Hobomok.

When they reached the chief's wigwam, they discovered that he was very weak and had lost his sight. Through Hobomok, Winslow was able to diagnose what was wrong and promptly administered a dose of medicine to Massasoit. Although not a qualified physician, he persisted in nursing the Chief and prepared medicinal potions. Slowly, Massasoit began to recover and re-gained his sight. It was thought the chief's illness had been caused through over-eating. News quickly spread around the settlement of Winslow's healing powers and Massasoit's recovery. This enhanced the Pilgrims' reputation amongst local Indians.

Massasoit warned Edward Winslow of an attack which was being planned by the Massachusett tribe on the colony at Wessagusset. Winslow lost no time in returning to the Plantation and, in any case, he had missed meeting the captain of the Dutch ship as it had been refloated. News of the planned attack was given to the Governor.

As a result, Captain Standish, along with eight others, set off on a reconnaissance visit in the shallop to find the *Swan* which was anchored in Boston Bay. On their arrival, the ship appeared to have been abandoned and there was no sign of any Wessagusset men on board. Muskets were fired towards the shore to attract their attention. Only then did the settlers appear. Standish instructed them to find a group of Indians with whom he could do business.

When they arrived at Wessagusset bringing goods for bartering with, the Indians appeared very hostile, brandishing knives. This angered Captain Standish and he was determined to teach them a lesson. He invited them to return on the morrow. This they did but the Englishmen were waiting for them. A knife was suddenly drawn by one of the Indians but Standish managed to wrestle it from the man and stabbed him. Two more Indians were killed and a youth was hanged. Their corpses were strung up on display for all to see outside the Wessagusset settlement.

The remaining Indians beat a hasty retreat leaving their womenfolk behind who were held as hostages. One was freed in order that she carry a message to the menfolk that the women would be killed if word of the incident was passed to other marauding tribes who might have similar ideas about attacking the settlement. Eventually Standish gave instructions for the women to be freed. He pointed out to the Wessagusset men just what had been achieved by so few settlers against a large body of Indians. He then offered them an alternative. They could either return with him to Plimoth Plantation or take their share of the corn which had been collected. The majority chose the latter. Most of them followed their leaders to Monhegan in the *Swan*. Some joined local fishermen, whilst others decided to return home to England. This episode appeared to be the beginning of the end of Thomas Weston's short-lived settlement at Wessagusset.

Before Captain Standish and his party left the ship to return to New Plymouth, they beheaded the Indian youth who had been hanged and kept his skull as a souvenir. For some years it was set on a pike at Plimoth Plantation as a warning to those who might be tempted to attack.

The remaining 60 or so settlers at Wessagusset deteriorated into an undisciplined, wild bunch with no scruples in their efforts to survive. It was not a good reflection on genuine settlers such as the Pilgrim Fathers who had arrived in the New World to work hard at starting a new life.

One day, the community at Plimoth Plantation received an unexpected visitor from England. He arrived in a fishing boat in New Plymouth Bay travelling incognito as a blacksmith. It was Thomas Weston in person. His original intention of coming to America was to check on the development of his own investment – the settlement at Wessagusset! When he had first landed, he had been attacked by Indians who stripped him of his clothing and belongings but he managed to escape with his life. He then reached Piscataqua (Portsmouth (F4), Rhode Island) and obtained food and clothing from some friendly fishermen before making his way to New Plymouth. Naturally, he was bitterly disappointed at the news that his settlement had disintegrated and asked the Governor if he could let him have a quantity of beaver skins to take back to England. He promised to repay this kindness but never did.

There was still a shortage of food in the colony and the Pilgrims kept a sharp eye on the horizon for any ship which might be carrying spare supplies. Two attempts were made to send a ship across the Atlantic from England to New Plymouth but both had to be abandoned because of stormy weather. The community could only wait patiently for the day when help would finally arrive.

CHAPTER 12

New Settlers

IN THE SUMMER OF 1623 an important letter arrived from Robert Cushman. Two more ships were about to depart from England bringing further settlers to the New World. Cushman's letter stated that they would be bringing more friends and relatives of existing settlers. In itself, this was something to look forward to.

Meanwhile, during the long hot summer of 1623, many crops began to wither and there was again a serious threat of famine. Neither did any other ships arrive from England or Holland with supplies. The Pilgrims got together and held a day of prayer. Before the end of the day, rain started to fall and became a torrent which lasted some days. The dried-up crops were revived. In the autumn the colony experienced an outstanding harvest. Again, 'the Lord had provided'.

The 140-ton ship *Anne* arrived accompanied by the 44-ton *Little James*. The total number of passengers on the vessels was 87. Of these 29 had come from Leiden and included Mrs. Samuel Fuller, wife of the physician; Mary and Sarah Priest; Thomas Morton Jnr; and Fear and Patience Brewster. Also in the party was Hester, wife of Francis Cooke with their three children. It must have been quite a re-union. There was also a widow called Alice Southward on board, destined to become the second wife of Governor Bradford, and a girl named Barbara, whose surname is unknown but who later married Captain Standish. The Pilgrims had hoped that John Robinson, their pastor in Leiden, might have arrived but they were disappointed. Perhaps he would join them later?

Not all the passengers were Separatists. There was a fair sprinkling of other folk – merchants, business people, craftsmen and others, some of whom would further enrich the Plimoth Plantation with their variety of skills and abilities. Despite their differences, they would still be subject to the governorship of William Bradford and would have to comply with the constitution of the plantation as laid down in the original Mayflower Compact and subsequent legislation.

Irrespective of the welcome given by existing settlers, many newcomers were sick and tired and perhaps disappointed when they saw the colony. The first observations of the newcomers were that the Pilgrims looked poorly dressed and poverty stricken. Houses seemed primitive, sleeping accommodation cramped and lacking in the home comforts they might have been used to in Holland or England. Quarrelling and thieving began to break out amongst the new arrivals and some of their number were critical of the Pilgrims for not working on the Sabbath day. Neither were some of them very happy about the barren landscape and remoteness of the region around Cape Cod Bay. They also complained of an unhealthy supply of drinking water.

In order to answer some of their queries and to try and pacify his new flock, the Governor decided to address everyone. He explained that the colony allowed for a diversity of religious tolerances and practices and, due to the absence of an ordained clergyman, members of the Plantation were still prevented from celebrating the sacraments. In answer to other questions, he stated that the Elders hoped to set up a school for children in the near future. Until such time as this happened, parents should be responsible for their own children's tutelage. For the time being, his answers were accepted.

When the *Anne* departed for England on 6 September 1623, the passenger list included Edward Winslow. He travelled back on the instructions of Governor Bradford to report to various bodies in England – including the Merchant Adventurers and the Separatist Church in England and Leiden – as to how the new colony was faring. This caused a vast amount of interest from people looking to start a new life across the Atlantic. There was then a clamber for patents and grants which, fortunately, did not affect the Plimoth Plantation. However, a patent was granted by Lord Sheffield to Robert Cushman and Edward Winslow on behalf of the colony which gave them authority to found a small town (New Plymouth).

By the following March, Winslow returned on the *Charity* accompanied by a new pastor, John Lyford, a former Anglican clergyman chosen by the Adventurers. Additional supplies were on board including food and a herd of cattle. By the spring of 1624, New Plymouth was a thriving settlement of over 30 cottages and various other buildings such as a community hall and school.

Naturally, although pleased to have a new pastor, the Pilgrims were bitterly disappointed that John Robinson had not come. Lyford tried his best to win them over but was lacking in personality. He soon became a close companion of John Oldham, a leading Nonconformist who had arrived in New Plymouth on board the *Anne* on its first trip. They began to consider themselves as official representatives of the Church and became arrogant. It was therefore not long before 'cracks' appeared in relationships between various religious groups, especially when Lyford began to adopt an Anglican approach to his ministry. This would have angered the various dissidents as it was exactly what they had rebelled against and the main reason for the setting-up of the Separatist Church in the first place.

Suspicion was rife as Lyford and Oldham spent long periods in composing letters. They asked the captain of the *Charity*, William Pierce, to carry these back to England on his return journey. However, having got wind of the situation, the Governor boarded the vessel and insisted that Pierce hand over the documents to him. The two men had been writing letters to the Church of England authorities and others, damning the good work and progress of the Plimoth Plantation and also declaring their intention to restore Anglicanism.

An enquiry was set up by the Governor and the two were brought before the Elders to account for their behaviour. They were accused of conspiring against the basic principles of the Plimoth community. Both were found guilty and sentenced to expulsion from the Plantation. Subsequently, Lyford moved to Nantasket (F23) then to Salem. He stayed there for a year or two until the arrival of further Puritan settlers when he moved on to Virginia. Oldham returned to New Plymouth in March 1625 and tried once again to persuade members of the Plantation to rebel. He was arrested and put aboard a boat which was about to leave for northern fishing grounds. He also ended up at Salem where he became a merchant.

By mid-1625 the Plymouth community was getting more established. Houses had been built and other buildings erected for various uses. Settlers had become more proficient at their respective tasks and family life continued, marriages took place and children were born. As in other Puritan settlements, they were governed by a strict moral code with severe punishment for unruly behaviour. Church attendance was compulsory and any form of entertainment banned on the Sabbath. There were also rules governing the wearing of modest clothing and obeying Elders.

In England some of the Merchant Adventurers, mostly Anglicans, on hearing of the way of life and religious practices adopted by the Pilgrims, decided to withdraw financial support. However, this meant that the Plimoth Plantation might be able to operate independently. Robert Cushman, siding with the Puritans, suggested they try and clear the outstanding debt of £1,400 which was still owed to their English sponsors. The ship *Little James* was loaded up with beaver skins and other goods and set sail for England. However, it was ambushed by a Turkish ship, and the captain and crew were kidnapped and transported to Turkey to be sold as slaves. The valuable furs were sold by the Turks.

Captain Standish left New Plymouth shortly after the *Little James* on another boat bound for England where he was to report on the progress of the Plimoth Plantation and act as representative for any trade transactions.

* * *

It was April of the following year before Captain Standish returned to the community with a plethora of bad news. Firstly, he had to report the death in Leiden on 1 March 1625 of John Robinson. He had been buried in the Pieterskerk where he is commemorated by a wall plaque. There was also the dreadful matter of the *Little James* and its crew. Thirdly, there were reports of a serious epidemic which had broken out in London with over 40,000 souls reported dead, including friends and relatives. Sadly, Robert Cushman had been one of them. In addition, King James I had died on 27 March 1625 and was succeeded by his second son, Charles I. This could be a mixed blessing for the Pilgrims Fathers.

Two years later, Isaac Allerton sailed to England to represent the Pilgrims to make an agreement with the Merchant Adventurers who had now gone into liquidation. The Adventurers agreed they would give up their rights and demands on the Pilgrims on condition that the outstanding loan was paid to them in nine annual instalments. This meant that, provided they kept up payments, the Pilgrim Fathers would have the sole right to everything in Plimoth Plantation. After long discussions, it was agreed that every single person in the colony would be included in any apportionment of land or property. The new agreement was signed by Allerton along with Governor Bradford and Captain Standish. It was their responsibility that the loan be repaid and a policy adopted regarding any trading or other business transactions.

Unfortunately, respected though he was, Isaac Allerton appears to have been unequal to the task of accounting and by 1631 finances were in a mess. The outstanding debt had by then risen to £6,000. Notwithstanding, in order to clear themselves of any more financial liability, Edward Winslow and the other two signatories bailed him out by selling off a substantial amount of their own land. Allerton left the Plantation and died at New Haven, New England in 1659.

An unfortunate incident occurred in the colony in 1630 when one of the passengers who came on the *Mayflower* was hanged for murder. John Billington, whose son had caused so much heartache and consternation amongst the Pilgrims when he wandered off into the woods, was accused of shooting a young man called John Newcomen. As a result, he was arrested and tried by a jury of twelve. He was found guilty and sentenced to death by hanging – the first execution to be carried out in Plimoth Plantation. Another sad experience for the Pilgrims.

* * *

Plimoth Colony was somewhat restricted. Land for farming was not good and the area was not very convenient for fishing and fur trading. The colony therefore remained quite small. By contrast, the area around Boston Bay was quickly developing as a more suitable place to settle. In 1629, a group of Puritans who set up the Massachusetts Bay Company received a charter granting stockholders or freemen the right to govern the colony. The town of Boston was then established.

In March 1630, the leader of a Puritan migration, John Winthrop, sailed into Salem harbour on the 350-ton *Arabella* accompanied by seven other ships. With him came nigh on 2,000 new settlers. In the following ten years 20,000 English people crossed the Atlantic to New England.

John Winthrop was born into a family of some substance at Edwardstone (B23), a hamlet not far from Sudbury (B22) in Suffolk. He lived with his large family at the ancestral home in nearby Groton for about 40 years and served as a Justice of the Peace. (The nearby town of Sudbury was in 1727 the birthplace of painter, Thomas Gainsborough, and his father's Regency-fronted Tudor House is now a museum.) Edwardstone has a small church with several brasses, whilst in St. Bartholomew's Church at Groton (B23) are brasses and memorials of Winthrop's ancestors and two of his four wives. Stained glass windows, bequeathed by American descendants, also commemorate both Winthrop and his son, John, who became a founder and Governor of Connecticut. Grandson Fitzjohn Winthrop, educated at Harvard, was also Governor of Connecticut. He was to return to Britain, joining Cromwell's army in Scotland and becoming Agent for Connecticut in London.

John Winthrop Snr. was a lawyer, educated at Trinity College, Cambridge, and London's Inner Temple. His first marriage took place in 1605 at the Church of St. Mary and All Saints, Great Stambridge (B19), Essex, and two of the Winthrop children were baptised there. The church has a commemorative stained glass window given by the American descendants of the Winthrop family. Like others before him, he converted to Nonconformism whilst at university and signed what was known as the Cambridge Agreement in 1629, the signatories of which swore they would emigrate to Massachusetts. He became the founder of Boston, New England and first Governor of Massachusetts, an office he was to hold on twelve occasions. In addition, he was the first President of the Commissioners of New England.

When Winthrop and his colleagues first sailed for the New World, they left behind a very discontented England. Economic prospects were poor as the Thirty Years' War was raging on the Continent causing large pile-ups at various ports of English goods including woollen cloth, a vital commodity in Britain's export trade. There was also much distrust of and opposition to Charles I who had authorised the torture and jailing of leading dissenters. Puritan reformers were imprisoned, fined and persecuted, leading many to seek asylum overseas to escape the terror gaining hold across the length and breadth of Britain.

As a consequence, many prominent men and women crossed the Atlantic. Some 45,000 emigrants journeyed to southern colonies and the West Indies whilst the remaining mass exodus was to New England. These included men such as John Cotton, England's leading Nonconformist minister from Boston, Lincolnshire, mentioned earlier in Chapter 4. There were also John Davenport, founder of New Haven colony; Thomas Hooker, founder of Connecticut; and Thomas Dudley, four times governor, thirteen times deputy governor of Boston Bay Colony and one of the first governors of Harvard. As more Puritans arrived from England, settlements spread throughout the north-east region of New England.

Boston, Massachusetts, soon emerged as the hub of New England's business, cultural and intellectual life. By the end of the 17th century, there were many well-to-do merchants there and in other places such as Salem and Newport. They had fine houses, servants and a very genteel lifestyle. Today, Boston still holds its place as the region's largest and most cosmopolitan city and is both attractive and historically fascinating. To stroll around some of the ancient suburbs along cobblestone streets past colonial-style houses, many retaining the air of bygone age, is an experience in itself. One of the most interesting of walks is the three-mile (five kilometres) 'Freedom Trail' which links sixteen of Boston's most historical sites, all of which played some role during the revolutionary era in the late 18th century. Along with Plimoth Plantation, Boston is considered by many people to have been the birthplace of American democracy and remains proud of its role in America's early struggle for independence. On the opposite side of the Charles River is the area known as Cambridge (F26), dominated by two of the world's most prestigious seats of learning – the Massachusetts Institute of Technology and Harvard University.

* * *

While Boston was rapidly developing as a major town, what was happening in Plimoth Plantation as the years progressed? Life went on very much as before. The Pilgrims continued in prayerfulness and observance of the Sabbath, helping others wherever they could. The good relationship they had built up with local Indians was maintained. In May 1630, another ship appeared in

New Plymouth harbour – the *Handmaid* – bringing 60 passengers from Leiden. This was to be one of the last groups of people to arrive from the Separatist Church who were thereafter referred to as 'The Pilgrim Fathers of New England.'

Edward Winslow on his trip to England circa 1638 was charged with finding another suitable minister for the church in New Plymouth. He located a Nonconformist clergyman named Jose Glover who agreed to take the post but, unfortunately, he died during the voyage. Winslow then managed to persuade another man of the cloth, the Reverend John Norton, a graduate of Peterhouse College, William Brewster's old college in Cambridge, to replace Glover. He stayed in the Plantation for a year but then moved on to the new settlement at Ipswich and in 1653 succeeded John Cotton as minister of the First Church of Boston. Eventually, another Cambridge graduate, the Reverend John Rayner, came to New Plymouth as minister and stayed eighteen years.

The 'father' of the colony and Ruling Elder of the Plymouth Church, William Brewster, died at Duxbury, New England on 18 April 1643 at the age of 77. From the early days in England and Holland, his religious tolerance, wise guidance and organisational influence had played a substantial role in the Separatist movement. He had also been one of the founders of Plimoth Plantation. William Bradford held the office of Governor of Plymouth colony until his death on 9 May 1657 at the age of 68, whilst Captain Miles Standish moved to Duxbury in 1632 where he died 24 years later. Plimoth Plantation's physician, Dr. Samuel Fuller, died in Plymouth at the age of 48, whilst Thomas Cushman, son of Robert, went on to become a freeman of Plymouth and, in 1636, married Isaac Allerton's daughter, Mary, by whom he had seven children. In 1649 he was elected as Ruling Elder of the Plymouth Church after the death of William Brewster. His wife, Mary, was the last surviving member of the *Mayflower* passengers when she died in 1699 at the age of 83. Edward Winslow eventually left Plymouth colony and returned to England where he served and supported the new Puritan government set up by Oliver Cromwell.

* * *

King Charles I held the firm belief that as monarch he ruled by divine right. This led to a major breakdown in his relations with Parliament and eventually to civil war. He was challenged in Parliament by Cromwell, a military leader, who entered the House of Commons in 1628 as MP for Huntingdon (B34), Cambridgeshire, the town of his birth. (At the time, the family home was at Hinchingbrooke House, Huntingdon. Cromwell and his family later lived for ten years at the vicarage in the nearby town of Ely (B32). He was a tythe collector for Ely Cathedral. His former school in Huntingdon is now a museum giving a fascinating insight into Cromwell's life.) Cromwell was a devout Puritan and in a major speech he openly condemned Popery and its rituals. He was later one of a number of Members of the House who refused to adjourn Parliament at the King's command. Charles dissolved Parliament and attempted to rule on his own.

In 1640, he was forced to re-convene Parliament which took the opportunity to assert an exclusive right to raise taxes. Two years later, the monarch declared war on Parliament and raised his standard at Nottingham (C13). The Civil Wars began which for four long years tormented the realm. Very roughly, the middle classes and merchants supported Parliament and the nobility and peasant class took the side of the King. The Royalist army suffered decisive defeats by Cromwellian forces at the battles of Marston Moor (1644) and Naseby (1645). (During the Civil Wars, Cromwell used the Falcon Inn in Huntingdon as his headquarters. His statue can be seen in the market square of nearby St. Ives (B34) in Cambridgeshire.) A year later, Charles surrendered himself to the Scots who handed him over to the English Parliamentarians (Roundheads). He was then held prisoner in Carisbrooke Castle (A14) on the Isle of Wight prior to standing trial in Westminster Hall in January 1649. Cromwell believed that the execution of Charles I was predestined by God and led the commission which tried and condemned him to death. With courage and dignity the King laid his head upon the block and was beheaded outside the Banqueting Hall in Whitehall on 30 January 1649.

From 1653 until his death five years later, Cromwell ruled England, Scotland and Ireland under the title of Lord Protector. Edward Winslow became one of his advisors and was responsible for carrying out new treaties being promoted by Cromwell to extend Britain's overseas territories. Whilst on one of these missions to Jamaica in the West Indies, Winslow died of a tropical disease in 1655 and was buried at sea.

When Cromwell died in 1658 he was succeeded by his son, Richard, who had no real interest in the office and the nation was controlled by a group of ambitious men. Then General Monck, one of Cromwell's best commanders, marched to London with an army and invited the exiled Prince Charles, son of the late King, to return to England and accept the throne as Charles II.

Oliver Cromwell had been buried in Westminster Abbey with all due pomp and ceremony but at the restoration of the monarchy in 1660 his body was disinterred and hanged at Tyburn (a site close to the where Marble Arch now stands in London). His head was stuck on a pole outside Westminster Hall. In 1960 his embalmed head was secretly buried in the ante-chapel of Sidney Sussex College in Cambridge, where Cromwell had been a graduate. There is a striking portrait of the Lord Protector in the college dining hall.

* * *

As the population of New England expanded and prospered, the Puritan clergy established Harvard College (F26) in 1636 with the specific aim of training young men for leadership of church, state and trade. It was the first college to be established in America and its main benefactor was an Englishmen – John Harvard.

Harvard was born in Southwark in 1607 where his father owned a butcher's shop, close to the present Southwark Cathedral, and the Queen's Head Inn on the site of the present 103 Borough High Street. His father and four of his brothers and sisters all died of a plague which swept London in 1625. John's mother died ten years later bequeathing to her son the Queen's Head, a part share in a house on Tower Hill and an amount of cash. Two years later, his surviving brother died, making him the sole beneficiary of the family properties and monies.

John was a clergyman, and he married Katherine Rogers, daughter of a master butcher, Thomas Rogers, who once owned a house in High Street, Stratford-upon-Avon (c3). It is a lovely black and white, half-timbered house, built in 1596, now named Harvard House, and was purchased in 1909 by Edward Morris of Chicago and donated by him to Harvard University. Displays in the house relate to its founder and his life and times.

John and Katherine Harvard emigrated to Boston, Massachusetts, in 1637. Harvard took with him over 400 books, mainly academic. Sadly, he died of consumption at the age of 30 in 1638. In his will there was a bequest to Harvard College of £1,700 and all his books. This led to the founding of a new college in Cambridge on the outskirts of Boston. In appreciation, the college authorities decided that the new institution be named after him. It subsequently became Harvard University. Its enrolment grew from the original twelve students to its current total of over 18,000 degree candidates.

Harvard developed as a modern university in the 19th century as professional schools were added to the original college. Its name, traditions and academic achievements have become world famous. The campus covers a large area with 500 buildings, including over 100 libraries and nine museums. Walking tours of the site are offered to visitors, details being available at the Information Office.

On the northern side of Boston Bay is the town of Salem (F27). It takes its name from the Hebrew word 'Shalom' meaning peace but it was rather ironic that intolerance and violence were two major aspects of this town in Puritan times. In 1626 Roger Conant and a small band of settlers arrived in Salem, formerly known as Naumkeag, after having spent three years at Cape Ann. They found the area around Salem to be more fertile and sheltered from Atlantic storms. In 1628, they were joined by John Endicott who arrived from England with the authority of Charles I to assume the role of Governor of the Massachusetts Bay settlement. Two years later, John Winthrop arrived to replace Endicott as governor and he moved the seat of government to Boston.

From its earliest days, Salem lacked religious tolerance and in 1636 an outspoken Congregationalist, Roger Williams, was hounded out of the place for challenging Puritan orthodoxy (see Chapter 14). Although they had started out in England as a persecuted group, the Puritans now became persecutors themselves. What had begun as a single-minded quest for religious freedom ended in intolerance. The New England Puritans were so convinced of their own beliefs that they refused to accept differences of opinion and persecuted other religious sects and banished them from their colonies. Persecution continued for most of the late 17th century and culminated in 1692. This dreadful period in Salem's history became known as the Witchcraft Trials.

It started when several young and impressionable girls, stirred by tales of voodoo from a West Indian slave, experienced convulsive fits and visions. This developed into hysteria. After examination, a local physician proclaimed they had become victims of 'the evil hand'. The slave, Tituba, and two other women were arrested and accused of witchcraft. The accusers claimed that the 'shapes and spectres' of certain friends and neighbours tormented them. The superstitions gathered momentum until at the infamous Witchcraft Trials over 200 persons were accused. When the 'witch hunt' began, nobody in the town was safe from being accused – 150 were imprisoned whilst nineteen innocent people were tried, found guilty and hanged.

Present-day Salem has much that recalls those days of terror and superstition. Firstly, there is Gallows Hill on which the hangings took place. Not to be missed is Pioneer Village which is a recreation of a 17th-century fishing village with period dwellings, wigwams, gardens and live animals. It is peopled by costumed guides who re-enact the lifestyles of the early settlers. Other attractions in the town include the Salem Witch Museum in Washington Square, presenting a vivid portrayal of the town and events leading up to and including the Witch Trials of 1692, using models and audio visual features.

There is also the Witch House at 310 Essex Street, the only home still standing in Salem with direct ties to the Witch Trials.

Again, guides are in period costume and tours of the house show daily living in a 17th-century community around 1692. On a similar theme is the Salem Witch Village in Derby Street. This was created and developed with the help of Salem's Witch Community and covers the origins of witchcraft. It takes the visitor on a journey back in time to discover myths and facts surrounding witches and their craft. If the visitor still thirsts for gory details there is the Witch Dungeon Museum on Lynde Street, close to the Witch House. This includes a re-enactment of the trial of beggar-woman 'Sarah Good' adapted from the original transcript.

Salem has a number of other attractions and is famous as the birthplace of literary giant, Nathaniel Hawthorne (1804-64). The area provided the inspiration and setting for many of his works including *The House of Seven Gables* and *Tanglewood Tales*. Alexander Bell lived in Salem when he invented the telephone and gave the first public demonstration of his new invention in 1877 at the Lyceum Hall in Church Street. At the heart of the downtown area around Essex Street, there is an atmosphere of the colonial era with brick walkways and a pedestrian mall. A number of shops devoted to the occult offer tarot and psychic readings and sell witchcraft and New Age items.

With the growth of population and commercial activity around Boston and the continuing arrival of new settlers, rapid expansion of new communities was taking place. As well as an influx of immigrants into Massachusetts, the other areas of New England – namely Maine, Rhode Island, Connecticut, Vermont and New Hampshire – were becoming populated. Many other European countries also founded colonies in North America. The French had settled in areas in what is now Canada and in Louisiana; the Dutch in New Amsterdam, which later became New York. The Swedes settled in Delaware, whilst the Spanish founded settlements in Texas, New Mexico, California and Florida. England then began to establish further plantations further to the south heralding a new wave of pioneers to American shores.

CHAPTER 13

Colonial Expansion

TWO DRIVING FORCES FUELLED the desire and need for British people to emigrate. Firstly, for freedom to worship in the way one wished; secondly, for commercial purposes by moving to a new country to make one's fortune. During the 16th and 17th centuries, emigration probably suited the monarchs who found the dissenters not only a challenge to their authority but also an embarrassment to the Established Church. Following the early Separatists and Puritans, other religious groups began to form in many parts of Britain. Seeking escape from persecution by bishops and clergy of the Anglican and Roman Catholic Churches, many left for the New World taking with them their religious beliefs and teachings. Some were important in either spreading the faith of their particular denomination or becoming leaders in colonial development.

One of the most influential men was George Fox who founded the Quakers. He was born in July 1624 at the hamlet of Fenny Drayton (C10) in Leicestershire where his father, Christopher, known as 'the righteous Christer', was a weaver and churchwarden. As an infant he had been baptised at the Church of St. Michael and All Angels, a lovely 12th-century Gothic church with Norman features in the little village of Fenny Drayton off the A5 east of Atherstone. It has much atmosphere, and information on its famous son is available inside the building. Sadly, the cottage where he was born was demolished many years ago but a monument was erected to his memory and commemorates the local link. It is a plain pyramidal shaft of mellow stone, about 15 feet (4.6 metres) in height and stands at the corner of George Fox Lane and Old Forge Yard.

In his youth, George Fox was taught the trade of shoemaking after which he moved to Mansfield (C15) in Nottinghamshire.

However, at the age of twenty, he gave his heart to preaching the Lord's Word and, in 1643, set out to meet other preachers across the country. In 1647, he was attracted to groups of Baptists and Congregationalists in Nottingham and, in their midst, began to form opinions and doctrines of his own which were to shape his future life. George was something of a mystic. He believed in the guidance of what he called 'an Inner Light' – a living contact with the divine Spirit. With rare courage and perseverance, he travelled the country, preaching and winning followers in many places. Naturally, his radical approach angered the church authorities and he was persecuted and thrown into prison on several occasions. In 1650, he was imprisoned in Derby County Jail for nearly a year on a charge of 'profanely addressing the church congregation after divine service'. He also served time in jail at Scarborough Castle (D25) in North Yorkshire for a similar offence.

His followers met regularly for worship on lines laid down by Fox and were called 'The Society of Friends'. To others, they became known as Quakers, possibly because of Fox's orders to a judge, Justice Bennet, 'to quake and tremble at the Word of the Lord' during his trial in Derby. This Christian sect was formally organised in 1667 and emphasised simplicity in all things. George Fox denounced war, formality in worship and the taking of oaths. He travelled through Wales and Scotland and later visited the West Indies, North America and Germany. *Fox's Journals* is considered by many as one of the world's greatest books. He died in London on 13 January 1691. He was buried at Bunhill Fields, a place of interment for Nonconformists such as John Bunyan, Isaac Watts, William Blake and Daniel Defoe, situated just off City Road in London and almost opposite to Wesley's Chapel.

* * *

By the time of his death, George Fox had established many Quaker meeting houses across the country. Many 'Friends' were successful business people, among them some of the prominent ironfounders during the Industrial Revolution. Other British Quakers in business included the families of such famous choco-late manufacturers as Cadbury, Fry, Terry and Rowntree. They first commenced production of chocolate with a view to offering a nutritious and wholesome drink for the poor.

Due to religious persecution, a number of 'Friends' emigrated to the new colonies on the eastern seaboard of North America. Some began to play a significant role in the establishment of new plantations and towns in vast and hitherto unpopulated areas. We shall look into the background of two such Quakers, one well known, the other not so.

* * *

Mahlon Stacye was born at Handsworth (D6), near Sheffield in South Yorkshire, and baptised at the local parish church of St. Mary's on 1 July 1638. The Stacye family lived at nearby Ballifield Hall (D6), a building which still survives but is much altered. It is situated just off the Worksop road and owned by the local council. After leaving school, Mahlon trained as a tanner. One day he heard George Fox preach a stirring message. It left a marked impression on the young lad and he started to attend meetings of the Society of Friends. They met in one another's houses until the building of a Quaker meeting house at nearby Woodhouse in 1665.

In 1668, Mahlon married Rebecca Ely from the town of Mansfield. They had five children. However, because of their Quaker beliefs, the family soon found life intolerable through the obstructions they encountered from Anglican Church authorities. After much thoughtful discussion and prayer, they decided to follow in the footsteps of earlier dissenters and emigrate to America.

Therefore, in 1678, Mahlon, Rebecca and their children, plus members of the Ely family, another named Revell, and other Quaker families, all set sail for the New World. They arrived on the east coast of America where the River Delaware enters the sea. The ship continued up the river until it reached a point where the tides would no longer take it, and they disembarked. Mahlon supervised the building of a wooden dwelling which later became a grist mill for the storage and processing of corn. He soon began to play a leading part in the establishment and organisation of a new colony in the vicinity. A settlement grew up around the mill.

Mahlon Stacye's Mill, Trenton, New Jersey

Eventually it became a town and, later, the City of Trenton, now the state capital of New Jersey. Trenton stands roughly midway between New York and Philadelphia and today has a population of over 400,000. Mahlon Stacye was considered to have been the founder of Trenton and the State House of New Jersey is named Ballifield after his birthplace in Sheffield. His name has since been incorporated into a number of Trenton's sites and buildings.

In 1714, a Philadelphian merchant, William Trent, bought 800 acres (3.23 square kilometres) from Stacye's son for a mill and summer home. He soon doubled his holdings and in 1721 laid out the streets of Trent's Town. The city began to develop as an early industrial centre and port on the River Delaware.

The New Jersey State Museum in Trenton encompasses a wide range of exhibits covering local culture from ancient archaeology to modern art. From the city's visitor centre, there is an interesting walk along historic Continental Lane to the Johnson Ferry House, a stone building which once served as George Washington's command post. It reflects the style and furnishings of an 18th-century Dutch farmhouse. Trent House at No. 15 Market Street, built in 1719, is an excellent example of Georgian architecture and is open to the public. It has been restored and furnished according to an original household inventory of 1726, depicting Colonial life at that time.

* * *

Perhaps the best known Quaker reformer and colonist was William Penn, founder of Pennsylvania and known for his 'Great Treaty' with the Delaware Indians. He named the colony as a tribute to his late father, Admiral Sir William Penn (1621-70). Sir William was a man of heroic stature who revolutionised naval warfare with his inventive tactics and strategies, all of which Horatio Nelson was to follow at the Battle of Trafalgar in 1805. Always sympathetic to the Royalist cause, Admiral Penn welcomed Charles II aboard a ship which restored the King to England and he was knighted on the deck.

His son, William Jnr., was born 'without a court adjoining London Wall' on 14 October 1644 and was baptised at All Hallows' Church, Tower Hill, London, where there is a tablet commemorating the event. (In the same church registers is the recording of the marriage of John Quincy Adams who became the sixth President of the USA). Much of William's childhood was spent at Wanstead (B15), Essex, and he was educated at Archbishop Harsnett's School at Chigwell (B16), now known as Chigwell School. The original school buildings of 1629 are still in use. (Opposite stands the tall King's Head Inn – the Maypole of Dickens' *Barnaby Rudge* where most of the novel is set.)

Penn was expelled from Christ Church College, Oxford, for Nonconformism (his portrait hangs in the Main Hall) and went to study law at Lincoln's Inn in London. His next move was to study in France at the Huguenot Academy of Saumur in the Loire Valley and, later, he helped manage his father's estates in Ireland. Though he was brought up by Anglican parents, after hearing the preaching of another famous evangelist in 1666, Thomas Loe, Penn converted to Quakerism. By then, he was in his early twenties and began to get involved with the Quaker cause. Penn was imprisoned for his radical campaigning on religious and personal rights, spending a period in the Tower of London. It was here he wrote the most enduring of his books – *No Cross, No Crown*. In 1672, William married Gulielma Maria Springett of Ringmer (B3), East Sussex, and five years later accompanied George Fox on a visit to America. Penn wrote a charter 'Concessions and Agreements' for a group of Quakers who were settling in the newly acquired territory of New Jersey (Mahlon Stacye was one of these). This charter, amongst other demands, provided for religious freedom as well as the right to trial by jury.

On William Penn's return to England in 1677, he lived at Warminghurst, Sussex. The house has now disappeared. Three miles south-east of Billingshurst (B1) is the little Quaker Meeting House of Coolham (B1). It is a timber-framed building with a stone-flagged floor and oak settles.

Despite his Quaker principles, Penn was over-extravagant in his spending and found himself in debt. In order to raise money he called in an outstanding debt of his father's which was owed him by Charles II. This took the form of a charter which he obtained on 4 March 1681. Through this, William Penn became the founder of Pennsylvania (meaning 'Penn's Woods') as a place where religious tolerance, understanding and personal equality could each be put into practice. Seventeen months later, William also acquired the right to sell tracts of land. He predicted the project would become 'the seed of a nation'.

When Penn and 100 followers set sail from England for the New World in September 1682, George Fox had a *bon voyage* message for them:

'My friends that are gone, and are going over to plant and make outward plantations in America, keep your own plantations in your hearts, with the spirit and power of God, that your own vines and lilies be not hurt.'

William stayed in Pennsylvania and governed the colony for two years until August 1684 when he returned to England. During this period he is understood to have signed a treaty with the Delaware Indians (Leni Lenape) at Shackamaxon (Philadelphia). Penn always respected the Indians' claim to their land and, in turn, his colony was never attacked during his lifetime. During the next twelve months, he completed at least another eight land transactions with the Delaware Indians. At the same time, he supervised the building of his mansion at Morrisville on the banks of the River Delaware, upstream from Philadelphia. He named it Pennsbury Manor. It is open to the public and run by the Pennsbury Society. The house faces the river over which Penn commuted to nearby Philadelphia by barge.

There was a dispute between Penn and the Roman Catholic governor of Maryland, Lord Baltimore, as to who should control the territory south of Pennsylvania. He returned to England to try and settle differences with Baltimore and found the country in a political and social fervour. He had supported James ii, but the Glorious Revolution of 1688 by the Dutch William of Orange brought William and Mary to the British throne, ruling on a joint basis. Four years later, Penn was suspected of treason and lost control of Pennsylvania until 1694. When his first wife died, he married Hannah Callowhill.

William Penn did not return to America until 1699 by which time Pennsylvania and Delaware had become two separate provinces. During his absence his original charter had proved unworkable and a further document was instituted by his former Secretary, William Markham, by now the Governor of Delaware. A more permanent charter was revised and finally agreed by William Penn in 1701. Later that year, due to further political turmoil in England, he went home, never to return to America. In 1712, William suffered an attack of apoplexy which caused his disablement. His wife, Hannah, took care of affairs. They lived at a residence, now demolished, at Field Ruscombe near Twyford (A15), Berkshire, where Penn died in 1718. After his wife's death in 1727, the proprietorship of Pennsylvania passed to their sons, John, Thomas and Richard.

From Field Ruscombe, William Penn's body was taken and buried in the little Quaker graveyard at Jordans (B14), Buckinghamshire, on 5 August 1718. Also buried there are his two wives and several children but the simple stone gravestones date only from the second half of the 19th century. The area has an interesting history, with roots stretching back to when William Penn and other Quaker notables held meetings at William Russell's farmhouse, now called 'Old Jordans'. The Friends Meeting House, a small brick-built building, was erected in 1688 near to the farmhouse. Curiously, in 1968, a vault containing the bodies of six children was discovered in the nearby 11th-century flint Church of the Holy Trinity on Church Road, Penn (B14). It is thought that they might be the remains of Penn's grandchildren.

Penn had allowed Christians of all denominations to settle in Pennsylvania and his colony welcomed those whom the Puritans had rejected. At last, he gave to American immigrants the religious freedom that had been promised. And when the colonies finally became independent states in 1776, freedom of worship was written into the American Constitution. In Philadelphia, a massive statue of William Penn stands high above the City Hall, dominating the city where he is still revered. The bronze effigy is 37 feet high (1.12 metres) and was modelled by Alexander Milne Calder. The statue was hoisted to the tower in sections, the work finally being completed on 28 November 1894.

※ ※ ※

During the mid-18th century, a group of Quakers in Manchester (D2), England, were called the Shaking Quakers because of the ecstatic dances they performed during their religious services. Later they became known simply as the 'Shakers'. By the end of the next century there was a total of nineteen Shaker communities in America. They shared a communal lifestyle based on the principals of common ownership of goods, equality of the sexes and pacifism. They also demanded celibacy of their followers which meant that the community was maintained through reliance on converts and taking in orphans and young children in the hope they would stay. One of the Shaker villages that has been preserved is at Canterbury in New Hampshire where 24 original buildings still stand. It is situated fifteen miles (24 kilometres) north of Concord.

※ ※ ※

It is wrong to assume that all British emigrants to the new

colonies in America were Nonconformists. People from other religious denominations sought a new life across the Atlantic for varying reasons. In particular, a large number of Roman Catholics settled in Maryland. Many lived in St. Mary's County, south of Washington, DC, situated on a peninsula bounded by the Potomac River on one side and Chesapeake Bay on the other. Maryland's first capital was St. Mary's City, site of the fourth permanent English settlement in the New World. Eventually the town disappeared when the capital was moved to Annapolis. However, a section has been recreated as 'Historic St. Mary's City', an 800-acre outdoor history museum with costumed guides and interpreters. It includes a reconstructed State House of 1676 and Assembly Hall where court cases are re-enacted. At nearby St. Inigoes is the fine Roman Catholic Church of St. Ignatius with magnificent stained glass windows. It has one of the oldest cemeteries in America.

In Virginia, England's largest colony in America, there are examples of early colonialism. For instance, the capital – Williamsburg – boasts the College of William and Mary, the second oldest college in the country. The Governor's Palace of 1708 to 1720, once home to seven British governors and Virginia's first two governors, has been restored along with its beautiful gardens. The Jamestown Settlement is another living history museum which depicts life in the town during early settlement years. It has replicas of three ships which brought early settlers, along with a re-created palisaded fort. Yorktown is the site of a famous defeat of the British in 1781 during the American Civil War. The Yorktown Victory Center is a battlefield museum and includes a recreated Continental Army encampment. Both Jamestown and Yorktown are connected to Williamsburg by the Colonial Parkway.

An excellent example of a living history museum which depicts life in New England at a later period than that of the early Pilgrims is Old Sturbridge Village (F2). It covers the period 1790 to 1840 and contains a series of historic houses, farm buildings and shops, some built around a common, which have been transferred from their original sites and re-built on the Sturbridge site. Interpreters wear costumes of the period and farm the land, cook and make tools and implements by traditional methods. The town of Sturbridge itself has been a stopping place for travellers since colonial days and still welcomes visitors today.

* * *

On 5 April 1649 Elihu Yale was born in Boston, New England, the second son of David Yale, a prosperous merchant, and his wife Ursula. David Yale became disillusioned with the attitude towards non-Puritans in Boston and in 1651 he decided to leave America and return to live at the family's ancestral home, Plâs Grono near Wrexham (C16), North Wales, which he had inherited from his father. His wife and children followed a year later. As the Wrexham area was mainly Puritan, they did not stay there for long and moved to London. David Yale became a wealthy merchant who was well able to afford to give his sons a classical education. Elihu went to a private school where he learned Latin and read theology books. After leaving school, he was anxious to pursue a career as an adventurer and entered the service of the East India Company as a clerk. In October 1671 Elihu was selected to become a 'writer' in India. The voyage took six months, and he arrived there on 23 June 1672. He stayed for 27 years returning to England in 1699 after a successful career which culminated in his becoming Governor of Fort George, Madras.

During his time in India, Elihu married Catherine Hynmer, a widow with four children whose former husband had left her a small fortune. This legacy helped Elihu with his dealings in precious stones and diamonds. His marriage to Catherine produced three daughters and one son who died in infancy. This left Elihu with no male heir. In 1689, Catherine decided to return to England with all the children. After Elihu's return to England in 1699 he and Catherine went their separate ways.

The last twenty years of his life were spent between Plâs Grono and his London residence in Queen Square, Great Ormond Street. He had become a very wealthy man. From his window at Plâs Gron he could see the magnificent tower of St. Giles' Church, Wrexham, where his father had been churchwarden. He became a benefactor and erected a gallery and provided a pulpit and other items. In 1713 it was suggested to Elihu that he send his books to Connecticut College in Saybrook, an institution founded in 1701 by several Harvard graduates. In 1716, the College was moved to New Haven, and Elihu Yale was persuaded to become its main benefactor. Two years later, it took his name and became Yale College (F1). Today, Yale is one of the foremost universities in the United States.

Elihu died at his London address on 8 July 1721 but, prior to his death, not only arranged to be buried in the churchyard at St. Giles', Wrexham, but also wrote his own epitaph:

'Born in America, in Europe bred,
In Africa travell'd and in Asia wed,
Where long he liv'd and thriv'd
In London dead'.

Elihu's benefaction of the College was reciprocated. In 1901 the graduates of Yale University paid for the restoration of the north porch of St. Giles' to commemorate their bi-centenary and also financed the restoration of the Yale tomb in 1968. In tribute to Elihu, a replica of the ornate church tower of St. Giles' was erected on the Yale campus and in 1918, a stone was taken from the Wrexham church tower for incorporation into that at Yale.

Plâs Grono has been demolished but the nearby stately mansion of Erddig (C16) has been lovingly restored by the National Trust and is open to the public. Just a few miles from Wrexham, off the A5104 is Plas yn Ial and the little church at Bryn Eglwys (C17) which contains the Yale Chapel.

If the visitor wishes to make a tour of Yale University at New Haven in Connecticut, they should first enquire at the Information Office, located at the grand Phelps Gateway of the Old Campus on College Street. There is much to see including the Art Gallery, the Centre of British Art and New Haven Green, a 16-acre (6 hectare) common surrounded by a trinity of churches constructed in the Gothic Revival, Georgian and Federal styles.

* * *

In the New World of the latter half of the 18th century, the

British Parliament's taxation policies were placing an increasing financial burden on the colonists. The New Englanders had no representative in Parliament in London. Angered by England's attitude and inspired by the oratory of such Puritan leaders as John Hancock, Samuel Adams, James Otis and Paul Revere – known as the Sons of Liberty – the colonists' passions ran high. The flames of rebellion were being fanned. It was to lead to the American Revolution and eventually culminate in the signing of the Declaration of Independence on 4 July 1776. The anniversary is commemorated as American Independence Day.

CHAPTER 14

Spreading the Gospel

ON THE RELIGIOUS FRONT, America was soon composed of many diverse traditions of the Christian faith: the Baptist and Puritan; the Quaker; the Lutheran which still followed the 16th-century doctrines of the Reformation; the Roman Catholic of liturgical worship (they had a large colony in Maryland); the Congregationalists – especially around New England; the Episcopalians of Virginia and the Carolinas; the Presbyterian, Dutch and German Reformed Churches; and the Anglicans who were rather in a minority. There were also the religions of the Black communities. In addition were the Jews, and others, who were attracted to the new country. All of these shaped the rich pattern of religion across America.

Baptists can trace their roots to Thomas Helwys, a Puritan, who returned to London from Amsterdam in 1611, inspired by the doctrines of John Smyth. He founded a church in Newgate Street, Spitalfields, and its distinctive belief was in believers' baptism, rather than infant baptism practised by the Established Church. Despite persecution, the Baptists continued to spread during the 17th century. During this time *The Pilgrims Progress* was written by a Baptist pastor, John Bunyan, whilst he was in Bedford prison.

The Baptist Church spread to America in 1636, with the founding of the community at Providence, Rhode Island by former Congregationalist Roger Williams. He had already spent some time in Plymouth, New England, when the Mayflower Compact was fresh in men's minds. Due to the intolerance of the Massachusetts Bay settlers who were mainly Puritans, Williams fled to Rhode Island to start his own colony. The denomination has grown to be one of the largest in America and was the origin of the black Baptist Church movement. The civil rights leader

Martin Luther King came from this branch; Billy Graham, whose evangelistic campaigns have taken place all over the world, also has an American Baptist background.

Another interesting parallel with the Pilgrim Fathers can be drawn concerning the arrival of the Methodists in the New World. Their story began in the little town of Epworth (D19) in North Lincolnshire, situated just a few miles from the villages where William Brewster, William Bradford and John Smyth originated. It was almost a century later that the Reverend Samuel Wesley was Rector of St. Andrew's Parish Church. He lived at nearby Epworth Old Rectory with his wife, Susannah, and their large family. The fifteenth child was John, born on 28 June 1703. His brother, Charles, was born four years later. In 1709, when John was only five, a disastrous fire broke out at the Old Rectory. The flames were beginning to consume the roof when it was discovered the John was still inside. He was rescued in the nick of time from an upper window, an incident in which his mother described him as 'a brand plucked from the burning'.

Francis Asbury preaching in the backwoods

John was sent to Charterhouse School in London and later to Oxford where he studied to become an Anglican priest at Christ Church College. He was ordained a deacon in Oxford Cathedral in 1725 and was later joined by his brother Charles. Six months later, John was made a Fellow of Lincoln College. John and Charles met a man of similar Nonconformist views to their own named George Whitefield who came from Gloucester (A21). George lived with his mother at the Old Bell Inn in Gloucester and worked as a pot boy and bar tender before going to Oxford. The family had worshipped at St. Mary de Crypt where Whitefield had been baptised. Often he would visit Gloucester Cathedral, an architectural gem of Norman origin and one of the finest ecclesiastical buildings in Europe.

The three young men found they had much in common and were influenced by Nonconformist preachers at Oxford. They met together for Bible study and prayer, aiming to live an orderly life and serve the poor. Like-minded students joined what they termed the Holy Club but, in mockery, others dubbed them 'Methodists' due to the methodical manner in which they conducted their lives.

In 1735 John and Charles set sail for the North American colony of Georgia to assist General Oglethorpe, a distinguished soldier and prison-reformer. He had agreed to undertake the organisation of a new colony, to be named Georgia, where the Wesleys hoped to become missionaries to the native American Indians. They spent much of their time around Savannah but the experience did not work out for either brother. Neither the new settlers nor the Indians wanted to live according to the rules of the Anglican Church. (Nearly four years later George Whitefield was also sent for a while to Georgia where he preached at every opportunity, organised schools and planned an orphanage. He returned to England but made a further visit to America, and he died in Massachusetts in 1770.) Feeling unfulfilled in their mission, the Wesley brothers decided to return to England in 1738. During the Atlantic voyage many storms were encountered but John noticed that a group on board from the Moravian Church in Germany showed no fear. He was astounded by their great faith.

On 24 May 1738 John went to a meeting in Aldersgate Street, London, and afterwards wrote in his journal that he 'felt his heart strangely warmed'. It was not long afterwards that he met up with George Whitefield again, now a rousing and celebrated preacher, who persuaded him to preach in the 'highways and byways' as well as in the churches. Due to his radical preaching, John not only angered the Church authorities but was refused the pulpit in many places. His work as an itinerant preacher took him the length and breadth of Britain, Ireland and the Channel Islands. During his lifetime, he is said to have travelled almost 250,000 miles, mainly on horseback until his latter years when he rode in a carriage.

In 1739 John bought a piece of land in the Broadmead, Bristol, where he built the first Methodist Chapel in the world – John Wesley's Chapel, affectionately known as the 'New Room', which was used as his headquarters. He also had a London base at the old Foundry in Moorfields which he used as a chapel. This was later replaced by a new chapel in City Road opened in 1778 – Wesley's Chapel – known as the 'Cathedral of World Methodism'. John's preaching was extremely popular with many, though he often suffered persecution during his early years (in 1773 the outbreak of opposition to his preaching in the Midlands came to be known as the 'Wednesbury Riots'). His appeal was very much to the working classes who were dissatisfied with the rigorous hold of Church of England clergy.

On 15 July 1779 John preached to his largest ever congregation on a weekday in the lovely Georgian Paradise Square in Sheffield. A plaque commemorating the event was unveiled in 1951 by the film magnate, J. Arthur Rank, a prominent Methodist.

In the basement of Wesley's Chapel in London is the Museum of Methodism and adjacent is Wesley's House, a mid-18th-century town house where John lived during the last eleven years of his life. He died there on 27 March 1791 at the age of 87 and his tomb is in the churchyard behind Wesley's Chapel, now sadly overshadowed by a modern office development.

The Old Rectory at Epworth is a fascinating place to visit and has much Wesley memorabilia. The rooms are full of character but perhaps of most interest is Susannah Wesley's kitchen where she taught her children. In the small town centre is the Red Lion pub where John often stayed, just opposite the market cross where he preached in the open. The parish church with its links with the Wesley family and the Wesley Memorial Church should be included in any visit. Both Wesley's Chapel in London and the New Room in Bristol are open to the public. At the New Room you can see the rooms used by the various circuit riders and preachers (including one dedicated to Francis Asbury – see below). About ten minutes walk away is the house of Charles Wesley at No. 4 Charles Street where he and his family lived between 1766 and 1771 and where he wrote some of his 7,000 hymns.

In August 1771 John Wesley was conducting one of his Methodist Conferences at the New Room in Bristol and appealed for preachers to go to America to 'spread the Gospel of Jesus Christ'. One of four who volunteered at the time was a young itinerant preacher named Francis Asbury. He was to be the founding father of the American Methodist Church and was inaugurated as its first Bishop. He came from a very simple background.

Francis Asbury was born in August 1745, the second child of Joseph and Elizabeth Asbury, at a cottage now gone without trace in Hamstead near Birmingham (C9) in the West Midlands. When Francis was only a few months old, the family moved to a cottage at the nearby hamlet of Newton, Great Barr, not far from West Bromwich (C8). It was to be the only home that he would ever know. Joseph Asbury was a farm labourer and gardener at Hamstead Hall. Elizabeth was a devout Christian and a major influence on her son's life. Bishop Asbury's Cottage, as it is known today, dates from the mid-17th century and is furnished with effects and furniture on permanent loan from the Victoria and Albert Museum in London. The cottage was earlier part of a short terrace, the other houses having been demolished some years ago to allow road widening.

Young Francis went to school at nearby Snails Green. He was a good scholar and able to read the Bible by the age of six. At the age of thirteen Francis was apprenticed to a Methodist blacksmith, Mr Foxall, at the Old Forge, now part of Forge Mill Farm just off Forge Lane, West Bromwich. His period of apprenticeship involved mainly manual work which built up his strength and physical stamina, both of which served him well in his future years as a circuit rider.

The Asbury family attended the parish churches at Great Barr and All Saints at West Bromwich (C8). At the time, the vicar of All Saints was the Reverend Edward Stillingfleet, a man of great

Methodist enthusiasm and friend of John Wesley. He encouraged Francis in his religious studies. The most powerful landowner in the area, the 2nd Earl of Dartmouth, was a relation of George Washington and another admirer of John Wesley. He also was influential in pointing Francis towards Nonconformist thinking.

In his early teens, the young Asbury attended a Methodist service at Hilltop near Wednesbury (C8). He was most impressed by the service and nature of the singing, prayer and sermon. At the age of eighteen he was converted and soon became a local preacher. His first sermon was preached at Manwoods Cottage which once stood just off Sandwell Park Lane on the present site of Manwoods golf course. In 1766 he left his work and became a full-time itinerant preacher, working in circuits in Staffordshire, Bedfordshire, Gloucestershire and – his final circuit – Wiltshire, mainly based in Salisbury.

It was in August 1771, whilst attending his first Methodist Conference in Bristol, that Francis Asbury took up John Wesley's challenge to go to America. After returning home to Great Barr to inform his parents of the undertaking, he set off on his long journey. The departure was an emotional one and Francis was never to see his parents again although he wrote to them regularly. On 4 September Francis Asbury set sail from the little port of Pill (A18) on the River Avon near Bristol, bound for the New World and a new life.

There are still various sites around the borough of Sandwell and the Black Country which relate to the Asbury story – Forge Mill Farm (the Old Forge); Sandwell Park Farm; the site of Manwoods Cottage; the Oak House at West Bromwich; All Saints Parish Church and the Manor House at Stone Cross. The fascinating Black Country Living Museum in Dudley houses a typical Methodist Chapel of the New Connexion, whilst Bishop Asbury's Cottage at Great Barr can be visited by prior application.

After crossing the Atlantic, Francis arrived in Philadelphia on 27 October 1771. On the following day, he preached his first sermon at St. George's Church, the oldest Methodist place of worship in America and the first to be called a Church. Many of the early preachers sent by Wesley were intimidated by the sheer scale and size of the American continent. They preferred to settle in the established centres such as Boston, New York and Philadelphia, making occasional trips into surrounding country. From the outset Asbury challenged this approach and, by example, became the first of a great army of circuit riders who were to spread the Gospel from the east coast of America westwards.

For more than 50 years Asbury knew no home except the road. A few months before his death, he told a British correspondent that his mailing address was simply 'America' – any postmaster would know that 'the man who rambled America' would in due course pass that way. Francis and his preachers went into every new community and nearly every log cabin in the wilderness. He was more widely travelled than any man of his generation and endured tremendous hardship, wading through swamps and swimming the rivers which flow from the eastern slopes of the Alleghenies and Appalachian Mountains. Normally, each of his travels took him twelve months over an area stretching between Florida and Maine.

Shortly after Asbury set sail for America, John Wesley realised that war with the Colonists was inevitable. He wrote to his preachers in America, urging them to control their tempers, to be moderate in their preaching and strive to be friends to all. It was only when the war broke out in 1775 that Wesley declared his support for the British Crown.

These views made Methodism very unpopular in America and many preachers returned home. Asbury remained – to provide the bridge between Methodism of the New World and the Old. Although he never did become an American citizen, Asbury was American in both sympathy and attachment. By 1778 he was the acknowledged leader of American Methodists. At the Baltimore Conference on 24 December 1784, Dr. Thomas Coke carried out the commission of John Wesley in ordaining Francis Asbury as a Bishop. The Methodist Episcopal Church was established.

Asbury suffered greatly from asthma and bronchitis in later years. His lifetime of toil and hardship eventually took its toll, and on 31 March 1816 in Spottsylvania, Virginia, he died. The funeral was held locally but, later, his body was moved to Baltimore to rest in a tomb at Eutew Street Church. In 1854 his body was once again moved to Mount Olivet Cemetery in Baltimore to a final resting place alongside the remains of other notable Methodist leaders.

During his lifetime the Methodist Church grew from around 1,000 to 200,000 members. He ordained over 3,000 preachers and preached 17,000 sermons. It is sad that so little is known about Francis Asbury, though he travelled a territory much greater than John Wesley and left as his monument a Church in America. Over 700 churches are named after him in America. In Washington DC, at the junction of 16th St. Columbia Road, stands an equestrian statue of the great circuit rider. On the plinth Asbury is described as 'The Prophet of the Long Road'. The monument was unveiled and presented to the nation by the President of the United States, Calvin Coolidge, in a ceremony on 16 October 1924. In paying tribute to Asbury, the President said:-

'He is entitled to rank as one of the builders of our nation....'

Adjacent to St. George's United Methodist Church in Philadelphia is a museum which includes many items of Asbury and Wesley memorabilia and other artefacts relating to early Methodist preachers. Application to view the interior of the church should be made at this building. There is also an equestrian statue of Bishop Francis Asbury in front of Drew University in New Jersey where the Methodist archives are kept for the nation.

'Tall oaks from little acorns grow.'

A Mighty Nation

THE STATUE OF LIBERTY, the symbol of American freedom and opportunity, stands on its island site in New York Harbour against the dramatic backdrop of the Manhattan skyline. Since it was erected and dedicated in 1886, the colossal monument has been a symbol for millions of people arriving in America to start a new life. They have come from all countries of the world in the hope of a better life than the one they left behind. It is a far cry from those early settlers and Pilgrim Fathers who arrived on the eastern seaboard to discover a hitherto unexplored land occupied only by native American Indians.

Few could have imagined when the *Mayflower* left Plymouth, England, on 6 September 1620 on its momentous voyage to Cape Cod, just what was about to begin. There is no doubt that the observation of strict discipline by the first Pilgrims and their strong faith played vital roles in their determination to win a better life for themselves and their descendants. Their insistence on starting off a new life by organising the first colony on democratic lines – as laid down in the Mayflower Compact – was a major reason for its success, despite illness, hazards, setbacks and attacks. Plimoth Plantation was, in fact, a role model for those who came afterwards.

Anyone in Britain wanting to know more about American history and the way of life at the other side of the Atlantic would do well to visit The American Museum. It is situated at Claverton Manor (A16) near Bath, Somerset, and was the first American museum to be established outside the United States. It was founded by Dallas Pratt and John Judkyn, two men with a deep appreciation of American arts and a desire to increase Anglo-American understanding.

The museum, which opened its doors in 1961, contains a

series of furnished rooms which range from the late 17th to mid-19th centuries and show the cultural traditions of English Puritans to the Spanish colonists of New Mexico. Many of the rooms are fitted with original panelling and floor boards brought from houses in the United States and reconstructed to present both the achievements of American craftsmen and a living picture of domestic life. After touring the house, take time to visit the cafeteria where you can sample traditional American cookies and other delights.

From those original thirteen colonies represented at the signing of the Declaration of Independence, the United States of America of today has fifty states. What was once an individualistic nation has changed into a democratic world power. It has become the leading nation in technological and scientific progress, not the least in the exploration of the Universe.

For the likes of William Brewster, William Bradford, Edward Winslow and other early pioneers, their strong faith in God helped them overcome all things. The Statue of Liberty proclaims the message – Libertè, Egalitè, Fraternitè (Liberty, Equality, Fraternity) – a symbol of a free and independent nation. And to quote the words of those early Pilgrim Fathers –

'THROUGH GOD – ALL THINGS ARE POSSIBLE'.

Useful Addresses

BRITAIN
Callers from overseas should remember to prefix the appropriate code for the United Kingdom before telephoning the following numbers:

The American Church in London
79a Tottenham Court Road
London W1P 9HB
Tel: 020 7580 2791

American Museum
Claverton Manor
Bath
North East Somerset BA2 7BD
Tel: 01225 460503

Bassetlaw Tourism Unit
Hundred Acre Lane
Carlton Forest
Worksop
Nottinghamshire S81 0TS
Tel: 01909 533484

Bristol Tourism
St. Nicholas Church
St. Nicholas Street
Bristol BS1 1UE
Tel: 0117 925 2748

British Tourist Authority
Thames Tower
Black's Road
Hammersmith
London W6 9EL
Tel: 020 8846 9000

Cambridgeshire Tourism
Shire Hall (Room 226)
Castle Hill
Cambridge CB3 0AP
Tel: 01223 717662

Chorley Tourism
Council Offices
Gillibrand Street
Chorley
Lancashire PR7 2EL
Tel: 01257 515300

Devon Tourism
County Hall
Exeter EX2 4QD
Tel: 01392 382176

East of England Tourist Board
Toppesfield Hall
Hadleigh
Suffolk IP7 5DN
Tel: 01473 822922

English Heritage
23 Savile Row
London W1X 1AB
Tel: 020 7973 3415

English Tourism Council
Thames Tower
Black's Road
Hammersmith
London W6 9EL
Tel 020 8563 3354

Essex Tourism
County Hall
Chelmsford,
Essex CM1 1QH
Tel: 01245 437547

Heart of England Tourist Board
Larkhill Road
Worcester WR5 2EZ
Tel: 01905 761100

Kent Tourism
Invicta House
County Hall
Maidstone
Kent ME14 2XX
Tel: 01622 696165

Lincolnshire Tourism
Lincoln Castle
Lincoln LN1 3AA
Tel: 01522 526450

London Tourist Board
Glen House
Stag Place
London SW1E 5LT
Tel: 020 7932 2000

The National Trust
36 Queen Anne's Gate
London SW1H 9AS
Tel: 020 7447 6700

Plymouth Marketing Bureau
Floor 7
Civic Centre
Plymouth PL1 2EW
Tel: 01752 261125

Southampton Cultural Services
Civic Centre
Southampton
Hampshire SO14 7LP
Tel: 023 8063 5904

South East England Tourist Board
The Old Brew House
Warwick Park
Tunbridge Wells
Kent TN22 5TU
Tel: 01892 540766

Southern Tourist Board
40 Chamberlayne Road
Eastleigh
Hampshire SO50 5JH
Tel: 023 8062 0006

West Country Tourist Board
60 St. David's Hill
Exeter EX4 4SY
Tel: 01392 425426

Wigan Heritage Service
The History Shop
Library Street
Wigan WN1 1NU
Tel: 01942 828128

Yorkshire Tourist Board
312 Tadcaster Road
York YO24 1GS
Tel: 01904 707961

HOLLAND

(UK prefix – 00 31)
(USA prefix – 011 31)

British Tourist Authority
Aurora Gebouw (5e)
Stadhouderskade 2
1054 ES, Amsterdam
Tel: 20 689 0002

VVV Amsterdam (Tourist Office)
Central Station
Stationsplein 10
Amsterdam
Tel: 20 6 340 34066

VVV Leiden (Tourist Office)
Stationsplein 210
2312 AR Leiden
Tel: 71 5 146 846

VVV Rotterdam
Coolsingel 67
Rotterdam
Tel: 10 6 340 34065

Leiden American Pilgrim Museum
Mandenmakerssteeg 11
2311 ED, Leiden
The Netherlands
Tel. 71 5 122 413

Netherlands Maritime Museum
Amsterdam
Kattenburgerplein 1
1018 KK Amsterdam
Tel. 20 5 232 222

USA
(UK prefix 00 1)

British Tourist Authority
625 North Michigan Avenue
Suite 1001
Chicago, Illinois 60611
Tel: (toll free) 1 (800) 462 2748

British Tourist Authority
7th Floor
551 Fifth Avenue
New York, New York 10176-0799
Tel: (toll free) 1 (800) 462 2748

Cape Cod Visitor Bureau
P.O. Box 790
Hyannis, Massachusetts 02601-0790
Tel: 508 362 3225

Harvard University
Events & Information Center
Holyoke Center
1350 Massachusetts Avenue
Cambridge, Massachusetts
Tel: 617 495 1573

Mayflower Society Museum
4 Winslow Street
Plymouth, Massachusetts 02361
Tel. 508 746 2590

New Jersey Division of Travel &
Tourism
CN 826
Trenton, New Jersey 08625
Tel: 609 292 6335

Philadelphia Visitors Bureau
1515 Market Street
Philadelphia, Pennsylvania
Tel: 215 636 3300
Pilgrim Hall Museum
75 Court Street
Plymouth, Massachusetts 02360
Tel. 508 746 1620

Pilgrim National Wax Museum
16 Carver Street
Plymouth, Massachusetts 02360
Tel. 508 746 6468

Plimoth Plantation
133 Warren Avenue, Rt. 3A
Plymouth, Massachusetts 02362
Tel. 508 746 1622

Plymouth County Visitors Bureau
Box 1620
Pembroke,
Massachusetts 02359-0579
Tel: 781 826 3136

Salem Witch Museum
Washington Square
Salem, Massachusetts 01970
Tel: 978 744 1692

Yale University
Phelps Gateway, 344 College St
New Haven, Connecticut
Tel: 203 432 2300

Bibliography

ANWYL, E. Catherine   John Smyth
(G.W. Belton Ltd., Gainsborough,
1991))

ASHE, Geoffrey   The Quest for America
(Pall Mall Press, London, 1971)

BANGS, Dr. Jeremy D.   Pilgrim Life in Leiden
(Leiden American Pilgrim Museum,
1997)

BATEMAN, Audrey   The Mayflower Connection
(Mickle Print Ltd., Canterbury,
1996)

BOARD, Joan   Pilgrim Country
(Happy Walking International Ltd.,
Matlock, 1998)

CAFFREY, Kate   The Mayflower
(Andrè Deutsch Ltd., London, 1975)

CHEETHAM, J. Keith   The Mayflower Trail
(Sheffield Publicity Department,
1985)

CHEETHAM, J. Keith   On the Trail of Mary Queen of Scots
(Luath Press Ltd., Edinburgh, 1999)

CROUCH, Marcus   Essex
(B.T. Batsford Ltd., London, 1969)

DAVEY, Cyril   John Wesley and the Methodists
(Marshall Pickering, Basingstoke,
1988)

DAVIES, Hunter — In Search of Columbus (Sinclair-Stevenson Ltd., London, 1991)

DOLBY, Malcolm — William Bradford of Austerfield (Doncaster Library & Information Services, 1991)

EASTERN COUNTIES TOURISM GROUP — Adventurers and Pilgrims (Lincolnshire Tourism, Lincoln, 1998)

ESSEX COUNTY COUNCIL — Stars and Stripes in Essex (Essex Tourism, Chelmsford, 1999)

HAMMOND, Peter — Sir Walter Raleigh (Pitkin Pictorials Ltd., London, 1978)

HARRIS, Donald F. — The More Children and the Mayflower (St. James Parish Church, Shipton, Shropshire, 1999)

HEATH, Dwight B. — A Journal of the Pilgrims at Plymouth (from 1622 original) (Corinth Books, New York, 1963)

HEATON, Vernon — The Mayflower (Webb & Bower Ltd., Exeter, 1980

JESSUP, Rev Edmund F. — The Mayflower Story (Whartons Ltd., Retford, 1977)

KETCHUM, Richard M. — The American Heritage (American Heritage Publishing Co, 1957)

KING, Jonathan   The Mayflower Miracle
(David & Charles, Newton Abbot,
1987)

LEWIS, H. Elvet   Homes and Haunts of the Pilgrim
Fathers
(The Religious Tract Society, 1920)

MALE, David A.   Christopher Jones and the
Mayflower Expedition
(Harwich Society, 1999)

NOBLE, Tony   Exploring Northamptonshire
Meridian Books, Oldbury, 1987)

PHILPOT, Don   Vermont, New Hampshire & Maine
(Moorland Publishing Co. Ltd.,
Ashbourne, 1995)

PRITCHARD, T.W.   Elihu Yale – the great Welsh
American
(Wrexham Area Civic Society, 1991)

SPURRELL, Rev. Mark   Boston Parish Church
(R.J.L. Smith & Associates, Much
Wenlock, 1996)

VERNON, Jennifer   Gainsborough Old Hall and the
Mayflower Pilgrim Story
(Friends of the Old Hall
Association, Gainsborough, 1991)

WINSLOW, Edward   Mourt's Relation
Corinth Books, New York, 1963

Some other books published by **LUATH** PRESS

ON THE TRAIL OF

On the Trail of Mary Queen of Scots

J. Keith Cheetham

ISBN 0 946487 50 2 PBK £7.99

Life dealt Mary Queen of Scots love, intrigue, betrayal and tragedy in generous measure.

On the Trail of Mary Queen of Scots traces the major events in the turbulent life of the beautiful, enigmatic queen whose romantic reign and tragic destiny exerts an undimmed fascination over 400 years after her execution.

Places of interest to visit – 99 in Scotland, 35 in England and 29 in France.

One general map and 6 location maps.

Line drawings and illustrations.

Simplified family tree of the royal houses of Tudor and Stuart.

Key sites include:

Linlithgow Palace – Mary's birthplace, now a magnificent ruin

Stirling Castle – where, only nine months old, Mary was crowned Queen of Scotland

Notre Dame Cathedral – where, aged fifteen, she married the future king of France

The Palace of Holyroodhouse – Rizzio, one of Mary's closest advisers, was murdered here and some say his blood still stains the spot where he was stabbed to death

Sheffield Castle – where for fourteen years she languished as prisoner of her cousin, Queen Elizabeth I

Fotheringhay – here Mary finally met her death on the executioner's block.

On the Trail of Mary Queen of Scots is for everyone interested in the life of perhaps the most romantic figure in Scotland's history; a thorough guide to places connected with Mary, it is also a guide to the complexities of her personal and public life.

'In my end is my beginning'
MARY QUEEN OF SCOTS

'...the woman behaves like the Whore of Babylon'
JOHN KNOX

Are there any surviving eyewitness accounts of Wallace?

How does Wallace influence the psyche of today's Scots?

On the Trail of William Wallace offers a refreshing insight into the life and heritage of the great Scots hero whose proud story is at the very heart of what it means to be Scottish.

Not concentrating simply on the hard historical facts of Wallace's life, the book also takes into account the real significance of Wallace and his effect on the ordinary Scot through the ages, manifested in the many sites where his memory is marked.

In trying to piece together the jigsaw of the reality of Wallace's life, David Ross weaves a subtle flow of new information with his own observations. His engaging, thoughtful and at times amusing narrative reads with the ease of a historical novel, complete with all the intrigue, treachery and romance required to hold the attention of the casual reader and still entice the more knowledgable historian.

74 places to visit in Scotland and the north of England

One general map and 3 location maps

Stirling and Falkirk battle plans

Wallace's route through London

Chapter on Wallace connections in North America and elsewhere

Reproductions of rarely seen illustrations

On the Trail of William Wallace will be enjoyed by anyone with an interest in Scotland, from the passing tourist to the most fervent nationalist. It is an encyclopaedia-cum-guide book, literally stuffed with fascinating titbits not usually on offer in the conventional history book.

David Ross is organiser of and historical adviser to the Society of William Wallace.

'Historians seem to think all there is to be known about Wallace has already been uncovered. Mr Ross has proved that Wallace studies are in fact in their infancy.'
ELSPETH KING, Director the the Stirling Smith Art Museum & Gallery, who annotated and introduced the recent Luath edition of *Blind Harry's Wallace*.

'Better the pen than the sword!'
RANDALL WALLACE, author of *Braveheart*, when asked by David Ross how it felt to be partly responsible for the freedom of a nation following the Devolution Referendum.

On the Trail of William Wallace

David R. Ross

ISBN 0 946487 47 2 PBK £7.99

How close to reality was *Braveheart*?

Where was Wallace actually born?

What was the relationship between Wallace and Bruce?

On the Trail of Robert the Bruce

David R. Ross

ISBN 0 946487 52 9 PBK £7.99

On the Trail of Robert the Bruce charts the story of Scotland's hero-king from his boyhood, through his days of indecision as Scotland suffered under the English yoke, to his assumption of the crown exact-

ly six months after the death of William Wallace. Here is the astonishing blow by blow account of how, against fearful odds, Bruce led the Scots to win their greatest ever victory. Bannockburn was not the end of the story. The war against English oppression lasted another fourteen years. Bruce lived just long enough to see his dreams of an independent Scotland come to fruition in 1328 with the signing of the Treaty of Edinburgh. The trail takes us to Bruce sites in Scotland, many of the little known and forgotten battle sites in northern England, and as far afield as the Bruce monuments in Andalusia and Jerusalem.

67 places to visit in Scotland and elsewhere.

One general map, 3 location maps and a map of Bruce-connected sites in Ireland.

Bannockburn battle plan.

Drawings and reproductions of rarely seen illustrations.

On the Trail of Robert the Bruce is not all blood and gore. It brings out the love and laughter, pain and passion of one of the great eras of Scottish history. Read it and you will understand why David Ross has never knowingly killed a spider in his life. Once again, he proves himself a master of the popular brand of hands-on history that made *On the Trail of William Wallace* so popular.

'David R. Ross is a proud patriot and unashamed romantic.'

SCOTLAND ON SUNDAY

'Robert the Bruce knew Scotland, knew every class of her people, as no man who ruled her before or since has done. It was he who asked of her a miracle - and she accomplished it.'

AGNES MUIR MACKENZIE

On the Trail of Queen Victoria in the Highlands

Ian R. Mitchell

ISBN 0 946487 79 0 UK £7.99

How many Munros did Queen Victoria bag? What 'essential services' did John Brown perform for Victoria? (and why was Albert always tired?) How many horses (to the nearest hundred) were needed to undertake a Royal Tour?

What happens when you send a Marxist on the tracks of Queen Victoria in the Highlands?

• you get a book somewhat more interesting than the usual run of the mill royalist biographies!

Ian R. Mitchell took up the challenge of attempting to write with critical empathy on the peregrina-

tions of Vikki Regina in the Highlands, and about her residence at Balmoral, through which a neo-feudal fairyland was created on Upper Deeside. The expeditions, social rituals and iconography of that world are explored and exploded from within, in what Mitchell terms a Bolshevisation of Balmorality. He follows in Victoria's footsteps throughout the Cairngorms and beyond, to the further reaches of the Highlands. On this journey, a grudging respect and even affection for Vikki ('the best of the bunch') emerges.

The book is designed to enable the armchair/motorised reader, or walker, to follow in the steps of the most widely-travelled royal personage in the Highlands since Bonnie Prince Charlie had wandered there a century earlier.

Index map and 12 detailed maps

21 walks in Victoria's footsteps

Rarely seen Washington Wilson photographs

Colour and black and white reproductions of contemporary paintings

On the Trail of Queen Victoria in the Highlands will also appeal to those with an interest in the social and cultural history of Scotland and the Highlands - and the author, ever-mindful of his own 'royalties', hopes the declining band of monarchists might also be persuaded to give the book a try. There has never been a book on Victoria like this. It is especially topical with the centenary of her death falling in 2001.

Mountain writer and historian. Joint winner of the Boardman-Tasker Prize for Mountain Literature in 1991, and winner of the Outdoor Writer's Guild's Outdoor Book of the Year award in 1999.

'entertaining and well researched... Mitchell, a distinguished historian with several books under his belt, writes with substantial first-hand experience of the rigors of walking in Scotland's more ot less trackless spaces' the times weekend

'...will give you much to think about next time you're up that mountain.' THE GUARDIAN, on Scotland's Mountains before the Mountaineers.

On the Trail of Robert Service

GW Lockhart

ISBN 0 946487 24 3 PBK £7.99

Robert Service is famed worldwide for his eye-witness verse-pictures of the Klondike gold-rush. As a war poet, his work outsold Owen and Sassoon, and he went on to become the world's first million selling poet. In search of adventure and new experiences, he emigrated from Scotland to Canada in 1890 where he was caught up in the aftermath of the raging gold fever. His vivid dramatic verse bring to life the wild, larger than life characters of the gold rush Yukon, their bar-room brawls, their lust for gold, their trigger-happy gambles with life and love. 'The Shooting of Dan McGrew' is perhaps his most famous poem:

> A bunch of the boys were whooping it up in the Malamute saloon;
> The kid that handles the music box was hitting a ragtime tune;
> Back of the bar in a solo game, sat Dangerous Dan McGrew,
> And watching his luck was his light o'love, the lady that's known as Lou.

His storytelling powers have brought Robert Service enduring fame, particularly in North America and Scotland where he is something of a cult figure.

Starting in Scotland, On the Trail of Robert Service follows Service as he wanders through British Columbia, Oregon, California, Mexico, Cuba, Tahiti, Russia, Turkey and the Balkans, finally 'settling' in France.

This revised edition includes an expanded selection of illustrations of scenes from the Klondike as well as several photographs from the family of Robert Service on his travels around the world.

Wallace Lockhart, an expert on Scottish traditional folk music and dance, is the author of Highland Balls & Village Halls and Fiddles & Folk. His relish for a well-told tale in popular vernacular led him to fall in love with the verse of Robert Service and write his biography.

'A fitting tribute to a remarkable man - a bank clerk who wanted to become a cowboy. It is hard to imagine a bank clerk writing such lines as:

> A bunch of boys were whooping it up...

The income from his writing actually exceeded his bank salary by a factor of five and he resigned to pursue a full time writing career.' Charles Munn,
THE SCOTTISH BANKER

'Robert Service claimed he wrote for those who would-nit be seen dead reading poetry. His was an almost unbelievably mobile life... Lockhart hangs on breathlessly, enthusiastically unearthing clues to the poet's life.' Ruth Thomas,
SCOTTISH BOOK COLLECTOR

'This enthralling biography will delight Service lovers in both the Old World and the New.' Marilyn Wright,
SCOTS INDEPENDENT

On the Trail of John Muir

Cherry Good

ISBN 0 946487 62 6 PBK £7.99

Follow the man who made the US go green. Confidant of presidents, father of American National Parks, trailblazer of world conservation and voted a Man of the Millennium in the US, John Muir's life and work is of continuing relevance. A man ahead of his time who saw the wilderness he loved threatened by industrialisation and determined to protect it, a crusade in which he was largely successful. His love of the wilderness began

at an early age and he was filled with wanderlust all his life.

'Only by going in silence, without baggage, can on truly get into the heart of the wilderness. All other travel is mere dust and hotels and baggage and chatter.' JOHN MUIR

Braving mosquitoes and black bears Cherry Good set herself on his trail – Dunbar, Scotland; Fountain Lake and Hickory Hill, Wisconsin; Yosemite Valley and the Sierra Nevada, California; the Grand Canyon, Arizona; Alaska; and Canada – to tell his story. John Muir was himself a prolific writer, and Good draws on his books, articles, letters and diaries to produce an account that is lively, intimate, humorous and anecdotal, and that provides refreshing new insights into the hero of world conservation.

John Muir chronology

General map plus 10 detailed maps covering the US, Canada and Scotland

Original colour photographs

Afterword advises on how to get involved

Conservation websites and addresses

Muir's importance has long been acknowledged in the US with over 200 sites of scenic beauty named after him. He was a Founder of The Sierra Club which now has over ½ million members. Due to the movement he started some 360 million acres of wilderness are now protected. This is a book which shows Muir not simply as a hero but as likeable humorous and self-effacing man of extraordinary vision.

'I do hope that those who read this book will burn with the same enthusiasm for John Muir which the author shows.'
WEST HIGHLAND FREE PRESS

On the Trail of Robert Burns

John Cairney

ISBN 0 946487 51 0 PBK £7.99

Is there anything new to say about Robert Burns?

John Cairney says it's time to trash Burns the Brand and come on the trail of the real Robert Burns. He is the best of travelling companions on this convivial, entertaining journey to the heart of the Burns story.

Internationally known as 'the face of Robert Burns', John Cairney believes that the traditional Burns tourist trail urgently needs to find a new direction. In an acting career spanning forty years he has often lived and breathed Robert Burns on stage. On the Trail of Robert Burns shows just how well he can get under the skin of a character. This fascinating journey around Scotland is a rediscovery of Scotland's national bard as a flesh and blood genius.

On the Trail of Robert Burns outlines five tours, mainly in Scotland. Key sites include:

Alloway - Burns' birthplace. 'Tam O' Shanter' draws on the witch-stories about Alloway Kirk first heard by Burns in his childhood.
Mossgiel - between 1784 and 1786 in a phenomenal burst of creativity Burns wrote some of his most memorable poems including 'Holy Willie's Prayer' and 'To a Mouse.'
Kilmarnock - the famous Kilmarnock edition of *Poems Chiefly in the Scottish Dialect* published in 1786.
Edinburgh - fame and Clarinda (among others) embraced him.
Dumfries - Burns died at the age of 37. The trail ends at the Burns mausoleum in St Michael's churchyard.

'For me an aim I never fash
I rhyme for fun'.
ROBERT BURNS

'My love affair on stage with Burns started in London in 1959. It was consumated on stage at the Traverse Theatre in Edinburgh in 1965 and has continued happily ever since'.

JOHN CAIRNEY

'The trail is expertly, touchingly and amusingly followed'. THE HERALD

On the Trail of Bonnie Prince Charlie

David R. Ross
ISBN 0 946487 68 5 PBK £7.99

 On the Trail of Bonnie Prince Charlie is the story of the Young Pretender. Born in Italy, grandson of James VII, at a time when the German house of Hanover was on the throne, his father was regarded by many as the righful king. Bonnie Prince Charlie's campaign to retake the throne in his father's name changed the fate of Scotland. The Jacobite movement was responsible for the '45 Uprising, one of the most decisive times in Scottish history. The suffering following the battle of Culloden in 1746 still evokes emotion. Charles' own journey immediately after Culloden is well known: hiding in the heather, escaping to Skye with Flora MacDonald. Little known of is his return to London in 1750 incognito, where he converted to Protestantism (he re-converted to Catholicism before he died and is buried in the Vatican). He was often unwelcome in Europe after the failure of the uprising and came to hate any mention of Scotland and his lost chance.

> 79 places to visit in Scotland and England
> One general map and 4 location maps
> Prestonpans, Clifton, Falkirk and Culloden battle plans
> Simplified family tree
> Rarely seen illustrations

Yet again popular historian David R. Ross brings

his own style to one of Scotland's most famous figures. Bonnie Prince Charlie is part of the folklore of Scotland. He brings forth feelings of antagonism from some and romanticism from others, but all agree on his legal right to the throne.

Knowing the story behind the place can bring the landscape to life. Take this book with you on your travels and follow the route taken by Charles' forces on their doomed march.

'Ross writes with an immediacy, a dynamism, that makes his subjects come alive on the page.'
DUNDEE COURIER

HISTORY

Blind Harry's Wallace

William Hamilton of Gilbertfield

Introduced by Elspeth King
ISBN 0 946487 43 X HBK £15.00
ISBN 0 946487 33 2 PBK £8.99

 The original story of the real braveheart, Sir William Wallace. Racy, blood on every page, violently anglo-phobic, grossly embellished, vulgar and disgusting, clumsy and stilted, a literary failure, a great epic.

Whatever the verdict on BLIND HARRY, this is the book which has done more than any other to frame the notion of Scotland's national identity. Despite its numerous 'historical inaccuracies', it remains the principal source for what we now know about the life of Wallace.

The novel and film *Braveheart* were based on the 1722 Hamilton edition of this epic poem. Burns, Wordsworth, Byron and others were greatly influenced by this version 'wherein the old obsolete words are rendered more intelligible', which is said to be the book, next to the Bible, most commonly found in Scottish households in the eighteenth century. Burns even admits to having 'borrowed... a couplet worthy of Homer' directly from Hamilton's version of BLIND HARRY to include in *'Scots wha hae'*.

Elspeth King, in her introduction to this, the first accessible edition of BLIND HARRY in verse form since 1859, draws parallels between the situation in Scotland at the time of Wallace and that in Bosnia and Chechnya in the 1990s. Seven hundred years to the day after the Battle of Stirling Bridge, the 'Settled Will of the Scottish People' was expressed in the devolution referendum of 11 September 1997. She describes this as a landmark opportunity for mature reflection on how the nation has been shaped, and sees BLIND HARRY'S WALLACE as an essential and compelling text for this purpose.

'A true bard of the people'.
TOM SCOTT, THE PENGUIN BOOK OF SCOTTISH VERSE, on Blind Harry.
'A more inventive writer than Shakespeare'.
RANDALL WALLACE
'The story of Wallace poured a Scottish prejudice in my

veins which will boil along until the floodgates of life shut in eternal rest'. ROBERT BURNS

'Hamilton's couplets are not the best poetry you will ever read, but they rattle along at a fair pace. In re-issuing this work, the publishers have re-opened the spring from which most of our conceptions of the Wallace legend come'.
SCOTLAND ON SUNDAY

'The return of Blind Harry's Wallace, a man who makes Mel look like a wimp'. THE SCOTSMAN

Reportage Scotland: History in the Making

Louise Yeoman

Foreword by Professor David Stevenson

ISBN 0 946487 61 8 PBK £9.99

Events – both major and minor – as seen and recorded by Scots throughout history.

Which king was murdered in a sewer?

What was Dr Fian's love magic?

Who was the half-roasted abbot?

Which cardinal was salted and put in a barrel?

Why did Lord Kitchener's niece try to blow up Burns's cottage?

The answers can all be found in this eclectic mix covering nearly 2000 years of Scottish history. Historian Louise Yeoman's rummage through the manuscript, book and newspaper archives of the National Library of Scotland has yielded an astonishing range of material from a letter to the king of the Picts to in Mary Queen of Scots' own account of the murder of David Riccio; from the execution of William Wallace to accounts of anti-poll tax actions and the opening of the new Scottish Parliament. The book takes pieces from the original French, Latin, Gaelic and Scots and makes them accessible to the general reader, often for the first time.

The result is compelling reading for anyone interested in the history that has made Scotland what it is today.

'Marvellously illuminating and wonderfully readable'.
Angus Calder, SCOTLAND ON SUNDAY

'A monumental achievement in drawing together such a rich historical harvest'
Chris Holme, THE HERALD

SOCIAL HISTORY

A Word for Scotland

Jack Campbell

with a foreword by Magnus Magnusson

ISBN 0 946487 48 0 PBK £12.99

'A word for Scotland' was Lord Beaver-brook's hope when he founded the Scottish Daily Express. That word for Scotland quickly became, and was for many years, the national newspaper of Scotland.

The pages of A Word For Scotland exude warmth and a wry sense of humour. Jack Campbell takes us behind the scenes to meet the larger-than-life characters and ordinary people who made and recorded the stories. Here we hear the stories behind the stories that hit the headlines in this great yarn of journalism in action.

It would be true to say 'all life is here'. From the Cheapside Street fire of which cost the lives of 19 Glasgow firemen, to the theft of the Stone of Destiny, to the lurid exploits of serial killer Peter Manuel, to encounters with world boxing champions Benny Lynch and Cassius Clay - this book offers telling glimpses of the characters, events, joy and tragedy which make up Scotland's story in the 20th century.

'As a rookie reporter you were proud to work on it and proud to be part of it - it was fine newspaper right at the heartbeat of Scotland.'
RONALD NEIL, Chief Executive of BBC Production, and a reporter on the Scottish Daily Express (1963-68)

'This book is a fascinating reminder of Scottish journalism in its heyday. It will be read avidly by those journalists who take pride in their profession – and should be compulsory reading for those who don't.'
JACK WEBSTER, columnist on The Herald and Scottish Daily Express journalist (1960-80)

The Crofting Years

Francis Thompson

ISBN 0 946487 06 5 PBK £6.95

Crofting is much more than a way of life. It is a storehouse of cultural, linguistic and moral values which holds together a scattered and struggling rural population. This book fills a blank in the written history of crofting over the last two centuries. Bloody conflicts and gunboat diplomacy, treachery, compassion, music and story: all figure in this mine of information on crofting in the Highlands and Islands of Scotland.

'I would recommend this book to all who are interested in the past, but even more so to those who are interested in the future survival of our way of life and culture'
STORNOWAY GAZETTE

'The book is a mine of information on many aspects of the past, among them the homes, the food, the music and the medicine of our crofting forebears.'
John M Macmillan, erstwhile CROFTERS COMMISSIONER FOR LEWIS AND HARRIS

Shale Voices

Alistair Findlay
foreword by Tam Dalyell MP
ISBN 0 946487 63 4 PBK £10.99
ISBN 0 946487 78 2 HBK £17.99

'He was at Addiewell oil works. Anyone goes in there is there for keeps.' JOE, Electrician

'There's shale from here to Ayr, you see.' DICK, a Drawer

'The way I describe it is, you're a coal miner and I'm a shale miner. You're a tramp and I'm a toff.' HARRY, a Drawer

'There were sixteen or eighteen Simpsons... ...She was having one every dividend we would say.' SISTERS, from Broxburn

Shale Voices offers a fascinating insight into shale mining, an industry that employed generations of Scots, had an impact on the social, political and cultural history of Scotland and gave birth to today's large oil companies. Author Alistair Findlay was born in the shale mining village of Winchburgh and is the fourth son of a shale miner, Bob Findlay, who became editor of the West Lothian Courier. Shale Voices combines oral history, local journalism and family history. The generations of communities involved in shale mining provide, in their own words, a unique documentation of the industry and its cultural and political impact.

Photographs, drawings, poetry and short stories make this a thought provoking and entertaining account. It is as much a joy to dip into and feast the eyes on as to read from cover to cover.

'Alistair Findlay has added a basic source material to the study of Scottish history that is invaluable and will be of great benefit to future generations. Scotland owes him a debt of gratitude for undertaking this work.' TAM DALYELL MP

FOLKLORE

The Supernatural Highlands

Francis Thompson
ISBN 0 946487 31 6 PBK £8.99

An authoritative exploration of the otherworld of the Highlander, happenings and beings hitherto thought to be outwith the ordinary forces of nature. A simple introduction to the way of life of rural Highland and Island communities, this new edition weaves a path through second sight, the evil eye, witchcraft, ghosts, fairies and other supernatural beings, offering new sight-lines on areas of belief once dismissed as folklore and superstition.

Scotland: Myth, Legend and Folklore

Stuart McHardy
ISBN: 0 946487 69 3 PBK 7.99

Who were the people who built the megaliths?

What great warriors sleep beneath the Hollow Hills?

Were the early Scottish saints just pagans in disguise?

Was King Arthur really Scottish?

When was Nessie first sighted?

This is a book about Scotland drawn from hundreds, if not thousands of years of story-telling. From the oral traditions of the Scots, Gaelic and Norse speakers of the past, it presents a new picture of who the Scottish are and where they come from. The stories that McHardy recounts may be hilarious, tragic, heroic, frightening or just plain bizzare, but they all provide an insight into a unique tradition of myth, legend and folklore that has marked both the language and landscape of Scotland.

Tall Tales from an Island

Peter Macnab
ISBN 0 946487 07 3 PBK £8.99

Peter Macnab was born and reared on Mull. He heard many of these tales as a lad, and others he has listened to in later years.

There are humorous tales, grim tales, witty tales, tales of witchcraft, tales of love, tales of heroism, tales of treachery, historical tales and tales of yesteryear.

A popular lecturer, broadcaster and writer, Peter Macnab is the author of a number of books and articles about Mull, the island he knows so intimately and loves so much. As he himself puts it in his introduction to this book 'I am of the unswerving opinion that nowhere else in the world will you find a better way of life, nor a finer people with whom to share it.'

'All islands, it seems, have a rich store of characters whose stories represent a kind of sub-culture without which island life would be that much poorer. Macnab has succeeded in giving the retelling of the stories a special Mull flavour, so much so that one can visualise the storytellers sitting on a bench outside the house with a few cronies, puffing on their pipes and listening with nodding approval.'

WEST HIGHLAND FREE PRESS

Tales from the North Coast

Alan Temperley
ISBN 0 946487 18 9 PBK £8.99

Seals and shipwrecks, witches and fairies, curses and clearances, fact and fantasy – the authentic tales in this collection come straight from the heart

of a small Highland community. Children and adults alike responsd to their timeless appeal. These *Tales of the North Coast* were collected in the early 1970s by Alan Temperley and young people at Farr Secondary School in Sutherland. All the stories were gathered from the area between the Kyle of Tongue and Strath Halladale, in scattered communities wonderfully rich in lore that had been passed on by word of mouth down the generations. This wide-ranging selection provides a satisying balance between intriguing tales of the supernatural and more everyday occurrences. The book also includes chilling eye-witness accounts of the notorious Strathnaver Clearances when tenants were given a few hours to pack up and get out of their homes, which were then burned to the ground.

Underlying the continuity through the generations, this new edition has a foreward by Jim Johnston, the head teacher at Farr, and includes the vigorous linocut images produced by the young people under the guidance of their art teacher, Elliot Rudie.

Since the original publication of this book, Alan Temperley has gone on to become a highly regarded writer for children.

'The general reader will find this book's spontaneity, its pictures by the children and its fun utterly charming.' SCOTTISH REVIEW

'An admirable book which should serve as an encouragement to other districts to gather what remains of their heritage of folk-tales.'
SCOTTISH EDUCATION JOURNAL

TRAVEL & LEISURE

Edinburgh and Leith Pub Guide
Stuart McHardy
ISBN 0 946487 80 4   PBK £4.95

You might be in Edinburgh to explore the closes and wynds of one of Europe's most beautiful cities, to sample the finest Scotch whiskies and to discover a rich Celtic heritage of traditional music and storytelling. Or you might be in Leith to get trashed. Either way, this is the guide for you.

With the able assistance of his long time drinking partner, 'the Man from Fife', Stuart McHardy has dragged his tired old frame around over two hundred pubs – all in the name of research, of course. Alongside drinking numerous pints, he has managed to compile enough historical anecdote and practical information to allow anyone with a sturdy liver to follow in his footsteps.

Although Stuart unashamedly gives top marks to his favourite haunts, he rates most highly those pubs that are original, distinctive and cater to the needs of their clientele. Be it domino league or play-station league, pina colada or a pint of heavy,

filled foccacia or mince and tatties, Stuart has found a decent pub that does it.

Over 200 pubs

12 pub trails plus maps

Helpful rating system

Brief guide to Scottish beers and whiskies

'The Man from Fife's wry take on each pub

Discover the answers to such essential questions as:

Which pubs are recommended by whisky wholesalers for sampling?

Where can you find a pub that has links with Bonnie Prince Charlie and Mary Queen of Scots?

Which pub serves kangaroo burgers?

Where can you go for a drop of mead in Edinburgh?

Which pub has a toy crocodile in pride of place behind the bar?

How has Stuart survived all these years?

Long familiar with Edinburgh and Leith's drinking dens, watering holes, shebeens and dens of iniquity, Stuart McHardy has penned a bible for the booze connoisseur. Whether you're here for Hogmanay, a Six Nations weekend, the Festival, just one evening or the rest of your life, this is the companion to slip in your pocket or handbag as you venture out in search of the craic.

Edinburgh's Historic Mile
Duncan Priddle
ISBN 0 946487 97 9   PBK £2.99

This ancient thoroughfare runs downwards and eastwards for just over a mile. Its narrow closes and wynds, each with a distinctive atmosphere and character, have their own stories to tell. From the looming fortress of the Castle at the top, to the Renaissance beauty of the palace at the bottom, every step along this ancient highway brings the city's past to life – a past both glorious and gory.

Written with all the knowledge and experience the Witchery Tours have gathered in 15 years, it is full of quirky, fun and fascinating stories that you wont find anywhere else.

Designed to fit easily in pocket or bag and with a comprehensive map on the back cover this is the perfect book to take on a walk in Edinburgh or read before you arrive.

FICTION

The Bannockburn Years
William Scott
ISBN 0 946487 34 0   PBK   £7.95

A present day Edinburgh solicitor stumbles across reference to a document of value to the Nation State of Scotland. He tracks down the document on the

Isle of Bute, a document which probes the real 'quaestiones' about nationhood and national identity. The document ends up being published, but is it authentic and does it matter? Almost 700 years on, these 'quaestiones' are still worth asking.

Written with pace and passion, William Scott has devised an intriguing vehicle to open up new ways of looking at the future of Scotland and its people. He presents an alternative interpretation of how the Battle of Bannockburn was fought, and through the Bannatyne manuscript he draws the reader into the minds of those involved.

Winner of the 1997 Constable Trophy, the premier award in Scotland for an unpublished novel, this book offers new insights to both the academic and the general reader which are sure to provoke further discussion and debate.

'A brilliant storyteller. I shall expect to see your name writ large hereafter.'

NIGEL TRANTER, October 1997.

'... a compulsive read.' PH Scott, THE SCOTSMAN

The Great Melnikov

Hugh Maclachlan

ISBN 0 946487 42 1   PBK £7.95

A well crafted, gripping novel, written in a style reminiscent of John Buchan and set in London and the Scottish Highlands during the First World War, The Great Melnikov is a dark tale of double-cross and deception. We first meet Melnikov, one-time star of the German circus, languishing as a down-and-out in Trafalgar Square. He soon finds himself drawn into a tortuous web of intrigue. He is a complex man whose personal struggle with alcoholism is an inner drama which parallels the tense twists and turns as a spy mystery unfolds. Melnikov's options are narrowing. The circle of threat is closing. Will Melnikov outwit the sinister enemy spy network? Can he summon the will and the wit to survive?

Hugh Maclachlan, in his first full length novel, demonstrates an undoubted ability to tell a good story well. His earlier stories have been broadcast on Radio Scotland, and he has the rare distinction of being shortlisted for the Macallan/Scotland on Sunday Short Story Competition two years in succession.

'... a satisfying rip-roarer of a thriller... an undeniable page turner, racing along to a suitably cinematic ending, richly descriptive yet clear and lean.'

THE SCOTSMAN

Grave Robbers

Robin Mitchell

ISBN 0 946487 72 3   PBK £7.95

After years of sleeping peacefully, the deceased dignitaries of Old Edinburgh are about to get a nasty surprise...

Grave-digger and funeral enthusiast Cameron Carter lives a relatively quiet life. Until a misplaced shovel cracks open a coffin lid and reveals a hidden fortune, that is. Nearly one hundred and seventy years after the trial of Scotland's notorious body snatchers, William Burke and William Hare, the ancient trade of grave robbing returns to the town's cemeteries.

Forming an unholy union with small time crook, Adam, Cameron is drawn into a web of crime that involves a bogus American Scholars' Society, chocolate chip ice cream and Steve McQueen. Their sacrilegious scheming doesn't go quite to plan, however, and events begin to spiral dangerously beyond Cameron the answers will be exhumed.

Will our hero pull the tour guide of his dreams?

Will his partner in crime ever shift those microwaves?

Is there an afterlife?

In Robin Mitchell's rude and darkly comic debut novel, all the answers will be exhumed.

'Good, unclean macabre fun from Robin Mitchell...'
IAN RANKIN

But n Ben A-Go-Go

Matthew Fitt

ISBN 0 946487 82 0   HBK £10.99

The year is 2090. Global flooding has left most of Scotland under water. The descendants of those who survived God's Flood live in a community of floating island parishes, known collectively as Port.

Port's citizens live in mortal fear of Senga, a supervirus whose victims are kept in a giant hospital warehouse in sealed capsules called Kists.

Paolo Broon is a low-ranking cyberjanny. His lifepartner, Nadia, lies forgotten and alone in Omega Kist 624 in the Rigo Imbeki Medical Center. When he receives an unexpected message from his radge criminal father to meet him at But n Ben A-Go-Go, Paolo's life is changed forever.

He must traverse VINE, Port and the Drylands and deal with rebel American tourists and crabbit Dundonian microchips to discover the truth about his family's past in order to free Nadia from the sair grip of the merciless Senga.

Set in a distinctly unbonnie future-Scotland, the novel's dangerous atmosphere and psychologically-malkied characters weave a tale that both chills and intrigues. In But n Ben A-Go-Go Matthew Fitt takes the allegedly dead language of Scots and energises it with a narrative that crackles and fizzes with life.

'*After an initial shock, readers of this sprightly and imaginative tale will begin to relish its verbal impetus, where a standard Lallans, laced with bits of Dundonian and Aberdonian, is stretched and skelped to meet the demands of cyberjannies and virtual hoorhooses.*

Eurobawbees, rooburgers, mutant kelpies, and titanic blooters from supertyphoons make sure that the Scottish peninsula is no more parochial than its language. I recommend an entertaining and ground-breaking book.'

EDWIN MORGAN

'*Matthew Fitt's instinctive use of Scots is spellbinding. This is an assured novel of real inventiveness. Be prepared to boldly go...*'

ELLIE McDONALD

'*Easier to read than Shakespeare – wice the fun.*'

DES DILLON

POETRY

Poems to be read aloud

Collected and with an introduction by Tom Atkinson

ISBN 0 946487 00 6 PBK £5.00

This personal collection of doggerel and verse ranging from the tear-jerking *Green Eye of the Yellow God* to the rarely printed, bawdy *Eskimo Nell* has a lively cult following. Much borrowed and rarely returned, this is a book for reading aloud in very good company, prefer-ably after a dram or twa. You are guaranteed a warm welcome if you arrive at a gathering with this little volume in your pocket.

The Luath Burns Companion

John Cairney

ISBN 1 84282 000 1 PBK £10.00

NEW SCOTLAND

Some Assembly Required: behind the scenes at the rebirth of the Scottish Parliament

Andy Wightman

ISBN 0 946487 84 7 PBK £7.99

Scotland - Land and Power the agenda for land reform

Andy Wightman

ISBN 0 946487 70 7 PBK £5.00

Old Scotland New Scotland

Jeff Fallow

ISBN 0 946487 40 5 PBK £6.99

Notes from the North Incorporating a Brief History of the Scots and the English

Emma Wood

ISBN 0 946487 46 4 PBK £8.99

LUATH GUIDES TO SCOTLAND

Mull and Iona: Highways and Byways

Peter Macnab

ISBN 0 946487 58 8 PBK £4.95

SouthWest Scotland

Tom Atkinson

ISBN 0 946487 04 9 PBK £4.95

The West Highlands: The Lonely Lands

Tom Atkinson

ISBN 0 946487 56 1 PBK £4.95

The Northern Highlands: The Empty Lands

Tom Atkinson

ISBN 0 946487 55 3 PBK £4.95

The North West Highlands: Roads to the Isles

Tom Atkinson

ISBN 0 946487 54 5 PBK £4.95

WALK WITH LUATH

Mountain Days & Bothy Nights

Dave Brown and Ian Mitchell

ISBN 0 946487 15 4 PBK £7.50

The Joy of Hillwalking

Ralph Storer

ISBN 0 946487 28 6 PBK £7.50

Scotland's Mountains before the Mountaineers

Ian Mitchell

ISBN 0 946487 39 1 PBK £9.99

LUATH WALKING GUIDES

Walks in the Cairngorms
Ernest Cross
ISBN 0 946487 09 X PBK £4.95

Short Walks in the Cairngorms
Ernest Cross
ISBN 0 946487 23 5 PBK £4.95

NATURAL SCOTLAND

Wild Scotland: The essential guide to finding the best of natural Scotland
James McCarthy
Photography by Laurie Campbell
ISBN 0 946487 37 5 PBK £7.50

'Nothing but Heather!'
Gerry Cambridge
ISBN 0 946487 49 9 PBK £15.00

Scotland Land and People An Inhabited Solitude
James McCarthy
ISBN 0 946487 57 X PBK £7.99

The Highland Geology Trail
John L Roberts
ISBN 0 946487 36 7 PBK £4.99

Rum: Nature's Island
Magnus Magnusson
ISBN 0 946487 32 4 PBK £7.95

Red Sky at Night
John Barrington
ISBN 0 946487 60 X PBK £8.99

Listen to the Trees
Don MacCaskill
ISBN 0 946487 65 0 PBK £9.99

BIOGRAPHY

Tobermory Teuchter: A first-hand account of life on Mull in the early years of the 20th century
Peter Macnab
ISBN 0 946487 41 3 PBK £7.99

The Last Lighthouse
Sharma Kraustopf
ISBN 0 946487 96 0 PBK £7.99

Bare Feet and Tackety Boots
Archie Cameron
ISBN 0 946487 17 0 PBK £7.95

Come Dungeons Dark
John Taylor Caldwell
ISBN 0 946487 19 7 PBK £6.95

MUSIC AND DANCE

Highland Balls and Village Halls
GW Lockhart
ISBN 0 946487 12 X PBK £6.95

Fiddles & Folk: A celebration of the re-emergence of Scotland's musical heritage
GW Lockhart
ISBN 0 946487 38 3 PBK £7.95

SPORT

Over the Top with the Tartan Army (Active Service 1992-97)
Andrew McArthur
ISBN 0 946487 45 6 PBK £7.99

Ski & Snowboard Scotland
Hilary Parke
ISBN 0 946487 35 9 PBK £6.99

Pilgrims in the Rough: St Andrews beyond the 19th hole
Michael Tobart
ISBN 0 946487 74 X PBK £7.99

CARTOONS

Broomie Law
Cinders McLeod
ISBN 0 946487 99 5 PBK £4.00

Luath Press Limited

committed to publishing well written books worth reading

LUATH PRESS takes its name from Robert Burns, whose little collie Luath (*Gael.,* swift or nimble) tripped up Jean Armour at a wedding and gave him the chance to speak to the woman who was to be his wife and the abiding love of his life. Burns called one of *The Twa Dogs* Luath after Cuchullin's hunting dog in *Ossian's Fingal*. Luath Press grew up in the heart of Burns country, and now resides a few steps up the road from Burns' first lodgings in Edinburgh's Royal Mile.

Luath offers you distinctive writing with a hint of unexpected pleasures.

Most UK and US bookshops either carry our books in stock or can order them for you. To order direct from us, please send a £sterling cheque, postal order, international money order or your credit card details (number, address of cardholder and expiry date) to us at the address below. Please add post and packing as follows: UK – £1.00 per delivery address; overseas surface mail – £2.50 per delivery address; overseas airmail – £3.50 for the first book to each delivery address, plus £1.00 for each additional book by airmail to the same address. If your order is a gift, we will happily enclose your card or message at no extra charge.

Luath Press Limited
543/2 Castlehill
The Royal Mile
Edinburgh EH1 2ND
Scotland
Telephone: 0131 225 4326 (24 hours)
Fax: 0131 225 4324
email: gavin.macdougall@luath.co.uk
Website: www.luath.co.uk